Anthony Giddens has been Lecturer in Sociology and Fellow of King's College, Cambridge, since 1969. He was previously Lecturer in Sociology at the University of Leicester.

His publications include *Capitalism and Modern Social Theory* (1971), *Politics and Sociology in the Thought of Max Weber* (1972), *The Class Structure of the Advanced Societies* (1973) and *New Rules of Sociological Method* (1976). He is also the editor of *Émile Durkheim: Selected Writings* (1972).

Modern Masters

Durkheim

Anthony Giddens

Fontana/Collins

First published in Fontana 1978
Second impression April 1980
Third impression October 1981

Copyright © Anthony Giddens 1978

Made and printed in Great Britain by
William Collins Sons & Co Ltd, Glasgow

A hardback edition of this book is
published by Harvester Press

Contents

Preface

The writings of Emile Durkheim have exerted an extraordinary influence over the development of modern social thought. In his own lifetime, Durkheim gathered around him an impressive array of talents, and his conception of social science became infused into a variety of disciplines through the activities of men such as Halbwachs, Mauss and Davy in sociology and anthropology; Simiand and Bourgin in political economy; Hubert in archaeology; Granet in Chinese studies; and through the work of Saussure in linguistics. The influence of the Durkheimian school in France was to some considerable degree undermined by the impact of the First World War. Halbwachs and Mauss remained dominant figures during the inter-war period, however, and continued the tradition of thought which Durkheim had established. Since the last war, the prestige of Durkheim in French social thought has weakened. On the other hand, his ideas have played a part, especially through their influence upon the writings of Piaget and Lévi-Strauss, in the rise of 'structuralism', which in one form or another holds a pre-eminent position in contemporary France.

In the English-speaking world, Durkheim has come to be regarded as the principal figure in the origins of 'functionalism'. Prior to his death, Durkheim's writings were well known to English-speaking authors in the social sciences; but for the most part they were not sympathetically received. *The Elementary Forms of the Religious Life* (1912), the last of Durkheim's major works, was the only one to appear in English while he was alive. The influence of Durkheim was first felt in British anthropology, largely as a result of the efforts of Radcliffe-Brown, who incorporated the substance of the former's standpoint within his own writings. As a result of a period spent teaching at the University of Chicago, Radcliffe-Brown also helped to stimulate a spread of interest in Durkheim's ideas in the United States. This was further expanded through the works of authors such as Talcott Parsons and Robert K. Merton; today the immediate influence of Durkheim probably remains stronger in the United States than anywhere else.

In this book, within a relatively limited compass, I have endeavoured to provide a comprehensive account of Durkheim's writings. In contrast to some other interpretations, I have attempted to show how strong their continuities are. I have also given some attention to showing the relevance of Durkheim's political views for the conception of sociology which he advocated. This conception of sociology today has to be regarded as seriously deficient. In the concluding chapter, I try to indicate some of the reasons why.

Introduction: Life and Work

Durkheim was not, as was Max Weber, his famous contemporary in Germany, an encyclopaedic thinker. What lends Durkheim's writings their intellectual power is rather his persistent attack upon a limited number of problems that occupied him throughout his intellectual career. In a general way, these are easily stated. One task that Durkheim set himself was the completion of an endeavour which he saw as initiated in the writings of Condorcet, Montesquieu and Comte before him: the establishment of sociology on an empirical basis. While these earlier writers had established the idea of a naturalistic study of society as a project, in Durkheim's view they had not managed to free themselves sufficiently from the philosophy of history to allow that project concrete realization. Durkheim preserved Comte's stress upon the autonomy of sociology as a distinctive field of study, trying to give more precision to the conception of sociological method which he believed this implied, and to demonstrate its application in empirical investigation.

A second concern of Durkheim was to tackle the issue of the significance of the rise of individualism in modern society. If the socio-political background to the writings of Max Weber was that of a failed revolution (1848), and the lack of a liberal centre in the German polity, Durkheim's was that of a successful revolution (1789), which however was not successful enough. That is to say, the ideals of liberal individualism proclaimed in the Revolution seemed at some considerable distance from the realities of nineteenth-century French society, and continued to be actively resisted by strongly entrenched forces on the Right. For such groups individualism was seen as a pathology, an expression of the decay of the cultural fabric. In *The Division of Labour in Society*, his doctoral dissertation and his first major published work, Durkheim tried to show the futility of condemnation of this sort: the ideals of individualism express the emergence of a new type of social order, which will increasingly transcend the traditional forms of society which the conservatives defended.

An absorption with the sources and nature of moral authority is a third theme that prevails throughout Durkheim's writings. In *The Division of Labour* he was concerned to show that the emergent form of society, based on 'organic solidarity', still necessarily involves the moralization of social relations, even if the new moral order contrasts radically with the old. He thus set out to criticize not only the conservative social philosophers, who wished to return to a type of moral order that had become obsolete, but also the utilitarian liberals, who held that the new society can and should be based purely upon exchange transactions. The conception of the 'isolated individual', entering into exchange relationships in order to maximize his personal returns, is itself, according to Durkheim, a product of social development and presupposes a moral order. In Durkheim's celebrated phrase, there is 'a non-contractual element in contract': the existence of contractual exchange presupposes moral authority, the authority which renders contracts binding.

Finally, Durkheim's works manifest an abiding

interest in the practical implications of social scientific knowledge. Durkheim's ideas in this regard have never been particularly popular among his subsequent interpreters, even among those who have been prepared to accept most of his other views. These ideas were nevertheless at the heart of Durkheim's concerns, and one cannot properly understand what he sought to achieve in his major works without reference to them. For Durkheim, the practical role of the sociologist is similar to that of the physician, who applies scientific findings to distinguish between sickness and health, to diagnose the causes of the former and develop remedial treatment for it. One of the aims of *The Division of Labour* was precisely this: to show that the spread of the ideals of individualism is not a symptom of a pathological condition of society, but on the contrary is the 'normal' and healthy expression of the social transformations that are engendering a new form of social solidarity. It was a diagnosis which Durkheim never abandoned, even if he later came to be dissatisfied with some aspects of his initial formulation of it.

Durkheim's life spanned a critical period of French and European history. He was born on 15 April 1858 at Epinal in the Lorraine, and died in 1917. He thus grew up in the aftermath of the French defeat in the Franco-Prussian War of 1870-1 and the bloody events of the Paris Commune. The final years of his life were overshadowed by the much broader confrontation into which the whole of Europe was plunged, and which threatened to destroy the social and economic progress that had been achieved in France in the intervening period. Durkheim was of Jewish extraction, and was brought up in an orthodox family; his father was a Chief Rabbi, and at one time Durkheim was expected to follow in his footsteps, for a while attending a rabbinical school. Although he decided to break with this family tradition, declaring himself agnostic, his personality remained strongly moulded by his early upbringing, and by the frugal and disciplined life of the household. In one of the few authoritative accounts of Durkheim's early life, Georges Davy remarks, 'the home, marked by austerity rather than opulence, in which observance of the law was both precept and example . . . produced in the young Lorrainian several ineradicable traits: scorn for the avoidance of effort, disdain for success accomplished without work, horror of everything that is not reliably founded . . .'[1]

At the age of eighteen, Durkheim went to Paris to study for entrance to the *Ecole Normale Supérieure*. He failed in his first two attempts to gain entry through the competitive examinations, but was successful at the third try. At the *Ecole* he was one of a brilliant group of intellectuals several of whom were to make a major impact upon cultural life and politics in France. Bergson and Jaurès were in the entry class preceding Durkheim; Janet and Brunot were members of the same cohort. Durkheim's interests soon became fixed in the area of social and political philosophy; according to Davy, from the beginning he insisted that all such philosophy should have directly practical implications. He was particularly hostile to what he saw as the superficial intellectual glitter that attracted certain of his contemporaries, some of whom in turn found him too unremittingly serious and austere. At the *Ecole*, Durkheim acquired political views, and a general attitude towards politics, which he kept to for the rest of his life. His political sympathies lay strongly with republicanism and progressive social reform, in the face of the reactionary sentiments of the monarchists and the Catholic Right; but he always opted to stay aloof from the *'cuisine politique'*, preferring to debate politics on the level of general principles.

Durkheim was later critical of the education he received at the *Ecole*, admitting the stimulus of its intense intellectual atmosphere but complaining that he learnt little of scientific developments occurring in psychology and the other human disciplines. In his formative years, he was influenced by Boutroux and Fustel de Coulanges, two of his teachers in the *Ecole* (the latter becoming its director in 1880). Through Boutroux, he was led to a close reading of Comte's works. But he also became interested in the philosophy of Kant, largely as a consequence of studying the writings of the neo-Kantian social philosopher, Renouvier. Kantian themes crop up frequently in Durkheim's works, and in *The Elementary Forms of the Religious Life* he was eventually to try to set out a systematic form of 'sociological Kantianism', as a theory of knowledge. Renouvier's philosophy became a strong influence on republican progressives, and Durkheim took over some of its emphases as his own. Renouvier stressed the importance of initiating a scientific and comparative study of morality, holding that scientific determinism is compatible with recognition of the autonomy of moral conduct; and he advocated the realization of liberal ideals through the activity of the state, co-ordinated through a programme of secular education.

Following his graduation, Durkheim taught philosophy in several provincial *lycées*, from 1882 to 1887. In between, he spent the academic year 1885-6 in Germany, studying contemporary developments in social philosophy and 'collective psychology' in that country.

On his return, he wrote two lengthy review articles, dealing with leading figures in German social thought. His sojourn in Germany served to consolidate and bring into more definite focus the emerging framework of his own ideas. He acquired there, as he subsequently remarked, a clearer 'sense of social reality, of its organic complexity and development'.[2] He had already, before leaving for Germany, made an initial formulation of what was to become *The Division of Labour*, and had come to see that the proper method of study of what he early on described as 'the relation between the individual personality and social solidarity' had to be sociological. The term 'sociology', coined by Comte, had fallen into disrepute with the declining reputation of Comte's work in the latter decades of the nineteenth century. Durkheim adopted the term only with some reluctance (a 'barbarous neologism', he later called it), and accepted that Comte's formulations were wanting: consequently, at the same time as he was preparing the materials for his doctoral dissertation, he was working on methodological issues in the social sciences.

The articles Durkheim wrote on German social thought helped him to obtain a post at the University of Bordeaux in 1887. The position, as a lecturer in social science and education, was established specifically for him, partly due to the influence of Louis Liard, the director of French higher education, who looked approvingly upon Durkheim's espousal of republicanism, and was himself a follower of Renouvier. In the same year, Durkheim married. He remained in Bordeaux for fifteen years, the most productive period of his life. In his inaugural lecture, he sketched an account of the prospects for sociology: sociology is a science that has just been born. Rather than debating its possibilities abstractly, we should get on with the process of inaugurating concrete sociological studies. Such studies can be applied to the elucidation of traditional philosophical problems, by recasting the latter in a more empirical light. This is true, for example, he argued, of moral or ethical issues. Moral phenomena have first of all to be studied scientifically, as 'systems of natural phenomena', before we can hope to resolve problems of how we should act morally. In contemporary times, he concluded, this task is one of urgent necessity. The moral hold of traditional values has become weakened; we must investigate the sources of moral authority that are now emerging, and show how they act counter to individual egoism.[8] His stance was militant: the influence of sociology can revitalize not only philosophy, but other affiliated disciplines such as history and law.

The Division of Labour appeared in 1893. Durkheim also wrote a secondary dissertation on Montesquieu that, following the format demanded by the French doctorate, was composed in Latin. In his public defence of his dissertations, Durkheim had to deal with some highly critical comments made by his examiners: Boutroux, who was one of them, and to whom Durkheim dedicated his work, had strong reservations about the claims of the primary thesis. Durkheim replied to the criticisms with vigour. His success in the examination seemed to many to be a triumph for sociology over the more reactionary positions in philosophy; sociology, as a contemporary reporter commented, 'won the right to be mentioned at the Sorbonne'.[4] Durkheim's imperialistic advocacy of sociology as the key social scientific discipline gained him as many enemies as friends, both in Bordeaux and in Paris. The exchanges

at his doctoral defence were the first of numerous
encounters with critics who rejected much or all of
Durkheim's conception of sociology. The sheer length of
time that Durkheim was forced to remain in Bordeaux
before finally being called to a chair in Paris is an index
of the opposition which his views provoked, intellect-
ually and politically. Publication of *The Rules of Sociological Method* (which appeared as a series of articles
in 1894, and in book form the following year) stimulated further controversy, as Durkheim intended it to
do, deliberately presenting the work as a bold sociological manifesto.

The Rules was followed in 1897 by *Suicide*, in which
Durkheim undertook to demonstrate the usefulness of
his notion of sociological method by applying it to a
specific empirical subject-matter. He had previously
published a statistical article on suicide, and had been
working on the subject over a period of some ten years,
concurrently with his other writings. While at Bordeaux
he also lectured in a variety of courses: on education,
the family, religion, and the history of socialism. He
undertook the latter course in 1895-6 partly as a response to some of his students who became influenced
by Marxism. He had first become directly acquainted
with Marx's works during his visit to Germany, but
had not previously studied Marx in any detail. By the
time he came to do so, most of his basic views were
well formed, and in his course of lectures, which were
apparently enthusiastically received by the students,
he tried to incorporate an interpretation of the origins
of Marxism, and of socialist thought more generally,
within his own system. Some critics have seen his
attitude towards socialism as ambivalent, but it was
really quite consistent and clear. He had no sympathy

with revolutionary Marxism, holding that revolutions change very little: profound change is always the result of long-term social evolution. He was favourably inclined towards reformist socialism, on the other hand, which he saw as compatible with his ideals of progressive social reconstruction. He rejected the thesis that the state is a medium of class domination: for him, the state on the contrary can and should serve as the vehicle for the realization of social reform, through furthering equality of opportunity.

With the exception of two pamphlets analysing the origins of German militarism, written during the First World War, the only study Durkheim ever published dealing with contemporary politics was an intervention in the public debate surrounding the Dreyfus affair. The article concerned ('L'Individualisme et les intellectuels', 1898) remained on a characteristically abstract level. It was written in response to the polemics of Brunetière, a conservative anti-Dreyfusard who had condemned the role of intellectuals seeking to lend their support to Dreyfus's case, as showing their disregard of traditional institutions, and purveying individualism and anarchy. As one such intellectual, Durkheim tried to give an interpretation of 'individualism', derived from his sociological ideas, which would refute the suggestion that it implies anarchy. No clearer exposition of Durkheim's standpoint, in fact, can be found in the whole of his writings. A distinction has to be drawn, he argued, between the conception of individualism that is expressed in utilitarianism' and classical political economy on the one hand, and the ideals of moral individualism which are produced by the process of social development on the other. The first of these, depending upon the notion of an isolated individual who by entering into exchange relations with others creates society, is indeed linked to the thesis that society can be reduced to the interplay of egoistic interests. But such a thesis, the expression of a particular philosophy, is quite different from individualism as a set of moral ideals, which Durkheim sometimes referred to generically as the 'cult of the individual'. Moral individualism is opposed to anarchic self-interest; it does not glorify the self, but on the contrary is oriented to the only moral values – those of freedom and equality – that, in modern times, can provide the basis of social solidarity.

In the same year that *Suicide* was published, Durkheim helped to found the famous review journal, *L'Année sociologique*; this occupied much of his time thenceforth until publication was suspended with the outbreak of the War. Although the policy of the *Année* was fairly eclectic from its beginning, the appearance of the journal, with its core group of collaborators, did more than anything to concretize Durkheim's sociology as a recognized 'school' of thought. The objectives of the *Année* were ambitious: to provide a comprehensive yearly review of sociological literature, and of related works in the 'specialized social sciences' of economics, demography, geography, ethics and law. The journal also undertook to publish occasional monographs and papers (several important pieces by Durkheim appeared in this format). The *Année* gave some particular prominence to works on the sociology of religion, to which Durkheim's interests turned increasingly in the latter part of his career. In this respect, according to his own testimony, his reading, in 1894-5, of the writings of some of the leading English and American ethnographers played a major role. He first encountered the works of these writers while teaching a course in religion at Bordeaux, and subsequently reviewed some of them in the *Année*. 'That course of 1895', he commented later, 'marked such a transition in the evolution of my thought that all my previous researches had to be taken up again to bring them in accord with these new insights.'[5]

The new insights were eventually embodied in *The Elementary Forms of the Religious Life*, but in the meantime, in 1902, Durkheim moved to a post in education at the Sorbonne, although he did not become a full professor there until 1906. Because the opening was in education, rather than sociology, he was at first reluctant to let his name go forward. Not until 1913 was his Chair made one in 'Education and Sociology'. Durkheim's predecessor in the position, Buisson, had played an important practical role, while a civil servant, in promoting the secularization of education in France. As one of his main responsibilities, Durkheim was charged with teaching a course on the history and theory of education in France, in which he gave an intellectual backing to the same ideals. This course was compulsory for all students undertaking the *agrégation* in arts and sciences, and through it Durkheim managed further to diffuse the influence of his ideas. The convergence between his sociology and the official ideology of republicanism was so great that some contemporary critics spoke caustically of the pervasive hold of 'State Durkheimianism' in the educational system.

These teaching duties, however, together with the burdens of the *Année*, retarded the progress of Durkheim's work on religion. *The Elementary Forms* did not appear until 1912. With the outbreak of hostilities in 1914, he immersed himself in the war effort, continuing his teaching while participating in numerous committees, concerned among other things with the production of papers and pamphlets on the war. His health was growing poor; his death at the early age of fifty-nine was undoubtedly hastened by the loss of his only son, André, in the Serbian retreat of 1915-16. André had already begun to show a definite intellectual virtuosity, and was becoming prominent among the more youthful members of the *Année* group. Durkheim's grief was so immense that for a while he could not work. He gradually resumed the demanding round of his activities, but towards the end of 1916 suffered a stroke. He made a partial recovery, but was left in a feeble state; he died on 15 November 1917.

A large part of the corpus of Durkheim's work, consisting mostly of lectures that he had written out for his various courses, was published posthumously. The most important of these are two studies of education (*Moral Education*; and his course at the Sorbonne on the history of the French educational system, published in two volumes as *L'Evolution pédagogique en France*); the Bordeaux lectures on socialism; a discussion of civic politics and the state (published in French under the title *Leçons de sociologie: physique des moeurs et du droit*, in English as *Professional Ethics and Civic Morals*); and an analysis of the philosophy of pragmatism, reconstructed from students' notes (*Pragmatisme et sociologie*).

1 Early Work: *The Division of Labour*

The arguments that Durkheim developed in *The Division of Labour* cannot be fully understood without some knowledge of the views they were directed against. The first such target was traditional moral philosophy. According to Durkheim, most moral philosophers have tried to resolve the problems of ethics by attempting to deduce ethical doctrines from *a priori* principles. But this, he argued, is a fruitless mode of procedure. What we must do instead is to study empirically the various forms of moral code that exist in different societies. 'Moral facts', Durkheim claimed, 'are phenomena like others; they consist of rules of action recognizable by certain distinctive characteristics. It must, then, be possible to observe them, describe them, classify them, and look for certain laws explaining them.'[1] If we see this, we then appreciate that moral codes are grounded in the social conditions of existence, such that the forms of morality appropriate to one society would be quite inappropriate in the context of another. The scientific study of moral conduct can disclose these conditions, and thereby show what are the moral codes demanded by any particular type of society. This is the method to be used when examining the rise of ideals of individualism.

On a more substantive level, Durkheim's polemics were aimed at two contrasting interpretations, offered by previous writers, of the significance of the growing complexity of the division of labour in contemporary society. One was that suggested by Spencer, and was the characteristic view of utilitarian philosophy more generally: the thesis that solidarity in the division of labour is produced automatically by each individual pursuing his own interests in economic exchange with others. I have already indicated why Durkheim repudiated this sort of standpoint: the prevalence of contractual exchange already presupposes a moral framework within which it is ordered, and hence the framework cannot be explained as the outcome of exchange. The other view which Durkheim was concerned to question was that expressed by Comte, among others. According to this conception, social solidarity always and everywhere necessitates the existence of a strongly formed *consensus universel*, or unity of moral belief. The implication of such a view is that the weakening of this consensus brings about a decline in social cohesion. Such was precisely the conclusion arrived at by conservative political thinkers and, Durkheim argued, is one reason why we find marked reactionary elements in Comte's nominally progressive philosophy.

The main ideas set out in *The Division of Labour* can be readily outlined against such a backdrop. An embracing moral consensus is indeed a necessary condition of social solidarity, Durkheim agreed: but only in the simpler societies, in which the development of the division of labour is still rudimentary. It is only one type of social cohesion, to which Durkheim gave the name 'mechanical solidarity'. As we approach modern times, it is increasingly displaced by a second type, 'organic solidarity'. This is indeed a form of cohesion based upon relationships of exchange, within a differentiated division of labour. But it cannot be understood as the natural outcome of self-interest. Rather, it expresses the emergence of new moral precepts: 'co-operation', Durkheim stressed, 'has its intrinsic morality.' (P. 228.)

In order to document the progression from mechanical to organic solidarity, Durkheim examined the development of systems of law. Moral phenomena do not easily lend themselves to precise observation. If we wish to study such phenomena 'according to the method of the positive sciences', we have to use an 'external index' (*fait extérieur*) whereby we can measure their evolution objectively. Legal codes provide such an index, because they are the formal expression of moral prescriptions. On some occasions, as Durkheim admitted, there may be disjunctions between laws and customary moral behaviour, as where a law is consistently ignored. But these are circumstances of transition, and if the changes in social conduct involved become stable and 'normal', the legal system soon becomes reorganized to bring it into line with the newly developing moral forms. Thus major changes in systems of law can allow us to plot basic transformations in the moral order of society.

All laws involve sanctions. Sanctions express the obligatory character of moral codes. Hence a classification of forms of law in terms of the types of sanction with which they are linked is a useful way in which to hope to identify different kinds of moral system. According to Durkheim, we observe two main contrasting types of sanction involved in legal codes. 'Repressive sanctions' are those associated with penal law: these consist in the inflicting of some form of suffering, such as loss of liberty or even loss of life, upon the transgressor. The second type, 'restitutive sanctions', characteristic of most areas of civil and commercial law, involve the restoration of the state of affairs which existed prior to the transgression of the law. The object of restitutive law is readjustment, or parity, rather than the punishment of crime. 'Crime', which mobilizes the moral sentiments of the community against the offender, is a phenomenon of penal law. A 'crime' can be thus regarded as any act that 'invokes against its author the characteristic reaction which we term punishment'. (P. 70.)

We cannot, according to Durkheim, define crime in terms of the *content* of a given class of actions, because the most diverse kinds of conduct, in different times and places, have been regarded as criminal. The only characteristic which crimes share in general is that they transgress moral beliefs that are strongly held collectively, and which thus call forth a punitive reaction from society. In restitutive law, each side of the legal commitment is usually clearly defined: that is to say, both the obligations which are involved, and the sanctions that are to be applied if these are not met, are spelled out. This is not the case in repressive law. Here the sanctions are specified, but not the moral beliefs to which these are oriented. Precisely because the latter are generally shared, and everyone knows what they are, there is no need for them to be formally enjoined in law. Thus the laws of homicide do not command us to respect life: they specify the sanctions against murder. It is often held that punishment exists primarily as a deterrent. Durkheim rejected this view, arguing that if this were the case, the sanctions applied in repressive law would not be graded according to how serious a crime is regarded, but according to the strength of motivations to the crime. Punishment is an act of vengeance on the part of the community: its ultimate source is the emotive response produced by the violation of deeply entrenched values.

The existence of repressive law hence manifests the prevalence of strongly held collective moral beliefs: in Durkheim's term, a *conscience collective* (which can be translated either as 'collective consciousness' or 'collective conscience', neither being particularly accurate renditions). It also follows, Durkheim went on to argue, that the greater the preponderance of repressive over restitutive law, the more unified and inclusive is the *conscience collective.* By this means, we can show that the *conscience collective* is most coherent and strong in the simplest forms of society: the relative prevalence of repressive law is an index of the pre-eminence of mechanical solidarity. In such societies, collective beliefs are centred in religion: 'in primitive societies, criminal law is regilious law.' (P. 92.) The most heinous crimes, those which are most severely sanctioned, are ones which contravene religious pre-scriptions. Those sorts of crimes which at a later period of social evolution come to be judged as the most serious (e.g., murder) have a relatively low rank in the simple societies. Where mechanical solidarity is the basis of social cohesion, social conduct is controlled by shared values and beliefs: the collectivity dominates the individual, and there is only a rudimentary develop-ment of individual self-consciousness.

The development of society in the direction of greater complexity in the division of labour correlates with the expansion of the role of restitutive law, and a progressive transition from mechanical to organic solidarity. Durkheim sought to encompass this process within an evolutionary scheme of increasing structural differentiation. The simplest type of human society takes the form of an aggregate: solidarity derives solely from communality of sentiment and belief. Like the cells of a simple organism, individuals are not connected by reciprocal ties; a society of this sort, because it is an aggregate rather than a system of mutually dependent elements, can shed part of itself without necessarily losing its unity, just as a cell can divide into separate and self-sufficient parts. The parts of the whole are connected 'mechanically', rather than forming an 'organic' unity as the parts of a differentiated biological (and social) system do. This type of social order is succeeded by one in which society becomes differentiated into segments, formed of kinship groups or clans. Here the level of individualism is still low, and property is still owned communally: private property has not yet made its appearance. Property is nothing more than the rights which individuals have over material objects; where the individual is strongly subordinated to the *conscience collective*, so also is the control of objects. Organic solidarity – that is to say, the interdependence of individuals or groups in systematic relations of exchange with one another – only begins to emerge in any significant sense with the development of specialization of production. For organic solidarity presupposes, not the similarity of individuals, but the growth of *differences* between them. There are two related historical preconditions of this: the separation of economic tasks from familial obligations, and the concentration of legitimate authority in the hands of a central agency (monarchical household or state). These processes are expressed in the rise of commercialism and the *Ständestaat* in post-medieval Europe, but receive a further major impetus through industrialization.

How are we to explain what brings about the increasing structural differentiation of society? Durkheim rejected the possibility of answering this question teleologically, as it seemed to him the utilitarians and political economists had tried to do. For them the expansion of the division of labour occurs because it increases the net sum of human happiness by maximizing the productivity of labour. But the progress of the division of labour, Durkheim asserted, does not inevitably increase human contentment. We can see this by the rising rates of suicide that are found in the European societies in the nineteenth century. The causes of growing social complexity have to be sought elsewhere. Durkheim found them in the influence of what he called 'dynamic' or 'moral density'. The crucial transition which has to be explained is that involving the disintegration of the segmental type of society: the latter must become significantly dissolved before a differentiated division of labour can appear, although once this has come into being it hastens the disappearance of segmental organization. The process of dissolution can only happen insofar as social relations are established between erstwhile separate clan groups: the 'moral gaps' between the segments have to become filled, or become of higher density. The process of the division of labour thus varies with moral density: and the main factor promoting growing moral density, in Durkheim's view, is population expansion, which forces erstwhile separate groups into contact with one another. In elaborating this thesis, Durkheim called upon a quasi-Darwinian metaphor. Among the animals, a growth in population density leads to specialization of function, so that different species are able to coexist; a similar principle applies in social evolution.

Durkheim tried to trace out in some detail the shrinking sphere occupied by repressive law in the judicial system, and the corresponding expansion of restitutive law. The latter does not replace the former in the same spheres in a direct and equivalent way, because the transfer from one type of law to the other expresses major changes in the alignment of the main institutions in society. Thus the transgression of religious sentiments gradually loses its character as a criminal act, so that it is not sanctioned by the state at all. Restitutive law, on the other hand, develops in substantial part to regulate the new areas of social conduct that are created by the development of the state, the occupational system, and other forms of secular association. Restitutive law consists of a reinstatement; it does not carry the same moral impulsion as repressive law. Punishment proportionate to the scale of the offence has no place here, nor has the concept of moral guilt. The idea of tolerating murder seems repugnant to us, because we feel it to be a crime; the question, on the other hand, of how much property a person is to be able to inherit from his parents is of a different character. The posing of the latter question, Durkheim accepted, will undoubtedly impinge upon a range of relevant moral considerations. But a process of litigation involved in, say, settling a dispute about the size of an estate, is not oriented to culpability and penal sanction – unless fraud should be involved. The latter type of possibility is in fact crucial to Durkheim's argument (relating back to his critique of Spencer): it shows that the functioning of restitutive law, and thus of organic solidarity, cannot become wholly detached from the influence of the *conscience collective*. A residuum of repressive law must continue to exist, regulating the moral codes necessary for the fulfilment of contracts and which, Durkheim went on to suggest, is centred upon respect for the autonomy, dignity and freedom of the individual, i.e., moral individualism.

Some critics have seen a major hiatus in Durkheim's reasoning in *The Division of Labour* at this point.[2] Did Durkheim imply that the *conscience collective* eventually disappears as mechanical solidarity is replaced by organic solidarity, or did he want to identify distinctive changes that occur in the *character* of moral codes in contemporary society? Certainly there are unresolved difficulties in Durkheim's argument – and he spent the rest of his intellectual career struggling with certain of them. But the main thesis of the book is clear enough, and does not involve an inconsistency. The two themes mentioned above are not mutually opposed, but closely connected parts of Durkheim's analysis. The process of the contraction of the scope of collectively held moral beliefs, which proceeds in direct relation with the social transformations bringing about, and wrought by, the growing complexity in the division of labour, is at the same time a process of transmutation of the content of such beliefs. It is just on this basis that the problem Durkheim first set out to examine – whether or not the morality of individualism expresses the needs of an emergent social order distinct from that of the past, or is a social pathology – is resolved in favour of the former. *The Division of Labour* contains an early version of the characteristic Durkheimian treatment of the relations between history, moral authority and human freedom. Freedom consists, not in escape from social forces and social bonds, but in the autonomy of action that

29

membership of society makes possible. In the simple societies, the dominance of the *conscience collective* limits the scope of individual action: this situation is transformed by the process of social development, not however by destroying moral authority, but by altering its form. The utilitarians and political economists correctly saw that the old type of moral solidarity becomes undermined with the course of social development, but they did not grasp the fact that the new type, organic solidarity, also presupposes the moral authority of society for its operation. They have treated freedom as 'a constitutive attribute of man', not as the product of history.

The Division of Labour carries a sting in the tail. The last section of the book, dealing with 'les formes anormales' of the division of labour, is quite short in relation to the rest of the book, and one might be forgiven for thinking of it as a minor addendum to the main thesis. But it is perhaps the most important part of the work, for in it Durkheim set out a symptomatology of the crisis of European culture, as he saw it, and the elements of a programme for social reform. His comments in this section of the book are fragmentary, and occasionally a bit obscure; but they embody a theory of class conflict, and of a classless society, which owe a good deal more to Saint-Simon than to Marx, and establish the framework within which he was later to try to account for the origins and significance of Marxism as a particular type of socialist doctrine. The term 'class' itself, however, hardly appears in *The Division of Labour*, and an adequate grasp of Durkheim's position demands an effort of reconstruction: in making such an effort, I shall not attempt to stay as close as I have done so far to the terminology Durkheim himself used.

Durkheim was not fond of the term 'industrial society', which Saint-Simon introduced into social thought, and he was critical of some of the latter's ideas. Nonetheless he drew quite heavily upon Saint-Simon, and there is an important continuity running from Saint-Simon, via Durkheim, to much more recent authors in sociology, who have elaborated something of a similar standpoint, which could be labelled generically the 'theory of industrial society'.[3] The theory of industrial society has been, I think, a long-standing alternative conception of class conflict and social transformation in the modern era to that offered by Marx : and it has, since Durkheim at least, provided an account of the nature and likely fate of Marxism itself.

The main elements of Durkheim's version of the theory of industrial society are as follows. The class struggles and tensions found in the development of nineteenth-century European societies do not indicate the appearance of a new form of class society (capitalism), but derive from the strains inherent in the transition from mechanical to organic solidarity. Class conflict expresses the incomplete realization of organic solidarity in the newly developing industrial order. Two kinds of connected change are necessary to complete the transition. One is the regulation of industrial bargaining, which is in a demoralized or *anomic* state because while the old form of moral authority, where every man 'knew his place' in a fixed hierarchy of things, has faded, the new order of moral individualism has not yet become fully established. The second is the completion of the processes of structural change initiated by the differentiation of the division of labour. The clashes of wage-labour and capital, according to Durkheim, derive from the conjunction of these two sets of (transitional) social conditions. Moral regulation of industry is demanded on two levels: on the level of the economy as a whole, and that of the occupational system itself. The first has to be achieved through the state, the second – as Durkheim argued after 1902 – through the development of 'occupational associations' or corporations (see pp. 60-2 below).

Many secondary discussions of Durkheim have emphasized his call for the moral regulation of industry, as the means of overcoming anomie, without sufficiently acknowledging the other social changes which he saw as integral to this. Organic solidarity presupposes social justice and equality of opportunity, or it cannot function 'normally'. Those societies in which mechanical solidarity predominated were hierarchially organized in terms of 'external inequalities', by which Durkheim meant inequalities deriving from the social circumstances of an individual's birth, such as aristocratic prerogatives and the hereditary transmission of private property. The first of these has been eradicated, and so must be the second. In organic solidarity, when fully developed, the only principle governing the distribution of social and material rewards which is consonant with the new moral order is that of 'internal inequalities', i.e., the differential distribution of talent and capacity. 'All external inequality', in Durkheim's words, 'compromises organic solidarity.' (P. 371.) Although Durkheim nowhere said so explicitly, it seems plain that this is a projection of an emerging classless society, if by 'classless' one means a society in which the concept of 'class' loses its application. The mature industrial order, as envisaged by Durkheim, is to be a differentiated one, laterally and hierarchially; after all, its foundation is the differentiated division of labour. But it will be a just society in the sense that equality of opportunity will prevail.

In *The Division of Labour*, Durkheim did not work out the consequences of this analysis for the future of Marxism and other forms of socialism. He was later (in his lecture-course on socialist ideas) able to do so quite easily. Socialism, like class conflict, is a product of the transitional phase prior to the maturity of organic solidarity: it is an expression, a symptom, of the strains thus brought about. Consequently, while socialist theories anticipate some of the needs of society, such as those for the moral regulation of industry and the alleviation of social injustice, they are not an accurate diagnosis of the social conditions which have produced them.

2 Sociological Method; its Application in *Suicide*

One of the objections which Durkheim's examiners raised against his doctoral dissertation was that it treated the evolution of morality as inexorably determined by social causes. Durkheim was quite explicit about it: the changes he tried to document in *The Division of Labour* are 'mechanically produced by necessary causes'.[1] He had no wish, he often stressed, to deny the distinctive character of society, as contrasted with the material world, insofar as the former clearly operates through human consciousness or ideas. Nonetheless, society is a part of nature, and a science of society has to be based upon the same logical principles as those which obtain in natural science. For Durkheim, the history of the origins of sociology is a history of its progressive freeing from abstract social philosophy. A variety of major thinkers, especially Montesquieu and Comte, have contributed to this process. Durkheim's subsidiary doctoral dissertation, on Montesquieu, makes it clear that Comte went substantially beyond his predecessor's achievements. After Montesquieu, 'No further progress could be made until it was established that the laws of societies are no different from those governing the rest of nature and that the method by which they are discovered is identical with that of the other sciences. This was Auguste Comte's contribution.'[2] But Comte nonetheless, Durkheim held, remained a philosopher; and, by applying dogmatically his 'law of the three stages' to the whole span of human social development, Comte tended to treat his work as a finalization of sociological knowledge rather than as just the initiation of a new science.

To set the science of sociology on a sound basis we have to abandon, according to Durkheim, the 'vague generalities' that abound in Comte's writings, while preserving their general standpoint. We must adopt the same reserve in the face of the subject-matter of sociology as the natural sciences do in regard to theirs: social reality cannot be grasped by anyone who refuses to plunge into the detailed empirical investigation of social life. Social facts, he affirmed boldly, must be treated as 'things' – perhaps the most controversial of the precepts advanced in *The Rules of Sociological Method*. This blunt affirmation that social phenomena belong to the realm of nature is introduced in the book in the context of a strongly Comtean interpretation of the progress of science. Empirical science has to conquer prejudice and illusion in man's ideas about nature before social conduct itself can be examined scientifically: the latter is an especially difficult accomplishment, for prejudice and illusion are actually part of our social life. To regard social facts as things is to perform the act of detachment necessary to recognize that society has an objective existence, independent of any particular one of us; hence it can be studied by methods of objective observation. The most important feature of a 'thing' is that it is not plastic to the will: a chair moves if pushed, but its resistance demonstrates that it exists externally to whoever is doing the pushing. The same is true of social facts, even if these are not visible in the way that a physical object like a chair is.

Social facts are external to individuals and exert constraint over them. In *The Rules*, pursuing the theme of the naturalistic character of sociology, Durkheim suggested that these characteristics of social facts closely parallel the externality of the physical world and the constraints or resistances which it offers to our actions – a position he later partly retreated from. Every individual is born into a society which is already organized, and which thereby moulds his personal development: a society may have a stable organization, in distinguishable respects, over several centuries, while generations of individuals live out their lives and die. An individual is therefore only one element in a totality, a single unit in a much larger system. The properties of the totality cannot be deduced from those of the individuals who combine to form it. The principle involved can be illuminated, Durkheim tried to show, by analogy with the combination of chemical entities. The properties of hydrogen and oxygen, considered in isolation, are quite different from those which appear when they combine as water. 'The hardness of bronze is not in the copper, the tin, or the lead which are its ingredients and which are soft and malleable bodies; it is in their mixture.'[3]

The constraining character of social facts derives from their external character, as does the constraining character of the physical world in which we move. The rules involved in contractual law, for example, are defined independently of the individual, and impose definite obligations upon him which he ignores or contravenes at his risk. A variety of other examples are proffered by Durkheim. A person may wish not to speak the language spoken by others in the community around him, or to use its system of currency: but his activities will be severely hampered if he does not do so. Similarly, an industrialist invites ruin if he ignores technical innovations which his competitors employ to manufacture their products more efficiently and cheaply than he can.

Durkheim later modified his original analysis of social constraint in important ways, which are presaged in *The Rules*, but not detailed there. The type case of social constraint is moral obligation. The constraints connected with the obligatory character of moral codes show a major difference compared to physical constraint, found in the character of the connection between an act and its sanction. Action in relation to the physical world conforms to what Durkheim called 'utilitarian prescriptions', in which the consequences of the individual's conduct flow directly from the nature of the act itself. A person who drinks water from a bracken pool risks being poisoned: the risk is inherent in the act of drinking such stagnant water. The same is not the case with the sanctions attaching to moral conduct, where the form and severity of the sanctions that may be called into play are not integral to the conduct itself, but derive (as indeed one might point out *The Division of Labour* already showed) from the sentiments which underpin the activity. One man kills another. The sanctions involved in such a circumstance are not immediately derivable from the act of killing itself; for in some circumstances the destruction of others is regarded as murder, and is stringently reproved, while in different circumstances it is regarded as an act of heroism, and thereby acclaimed.

In his hierarchy of the sciences, Comte ignored psychology: the science closest to sociology, and the one immediately below it in the hierarchy, is biology. Durkheim could not adopt such a dismissive attitude, since in his time psychology was developing rapidly as an experimental science. He studied the writings of some of the leading figures involved in these developments in Germany, and was much impressed by Wundt's psychological laboratory (he also included a lengthy analysis of the latter's more philosophical writings in his articles on German social thought). But he was as insistent upon the disciplinary autonomy of sociology as Comte had been before him. The external and constraining character of social facts separates them clearly from the subject-matter of psychology. Durkheim had, however, a divided attitude towards authors such as Wundt, who mixed a predilection for experimental psychophysics with the production of treatises on so-called 'collective psychology', which was effectively an anthropology of culture. The two sorts of enterprise seemed to Durkheim to be very distinct. He agreed that if 'collective' or 'social psychology' refers to the second of these types of endeavour, there would be no hindrance to substituting these for the term 'sociology': for the study of social consciousness is a central task of sociology. He also acknowledged the legitimacy and the importance of the formation of a 'positive science' of psychology. But such a science studies the characteristics of the individual as an isolated actor, and hence cannot explain properties deriving from the association of individuals in society. Sociology is a science *sui generis*.

Social facts, then, have to be explained in terms of other social facts. Durkheim distinguished two types of explanation that may be undertaken in sociology: the causal and functional. Each has to be clearly separated from psychological reductionism, which especially threatens to undermine functional explanation, since the latter involves a conception of 'needs' – but these are the needs of society, not those of individuals. Durkheim emphasized this point firmly. In his view, many prominent social thinkers had interpreted society solely as a medium for the satisfaction of individual needs, thus deriving society from some sort of conception of human nature. But this is a mistaken approach. 'Collective beliefs, emotions and tendencies are not caused by certain states of consciousness of individuals but by the conditions in which the social group in its totality is placed.' (P. 106.) A psychological training is certainly valuable for the social scientist, but only in order for him to be able to complement and expand upon the results of his sociological investigations. 'There is between psychology and sociology the same break in continuity as between biology and the physicochemical sciences. Consequently, every time that a social phenomenon is directly explained by a psychological phenomenon, we may be sure that the explanation is false.' (P. 104.)

Durkheim's discussion of functional and causal explanation in sociology in *The Rules* has been remarkably influential, although it is quite cursory. 'Function', he argued, must be clearly distinguished from 'intention' or 'purpose'. The intentions individuals may have in undertaking a given form of social conduct are likely to be discrepant from the function which that conduct fulfils in society: people go to Church to worship God, but the function of their activity is to enhance social unity. The function of a social item refers, in Durkheim's phrase, to its correspondence with 'the general needs of the social organism'. Thus, taking an example

from *The Division of Labour*, the function of repressive
sanctions is to protect and thereby sustain the values
of the *conscience collective*. Causal explanation, by
contrast, involves the identification of laws which explain the succession of social phenomena : an instance
would be the explanation of the relation between
moral density and the growth of the division of labour.
The causes of the development of a social form have to
be identified separately from the function it fulfils,
although any adequate explanatory account has eventually to combine the two.

Durkheim's conception of functional analysis is
closely connected to his attempt to provide criteria
for distinguishing social normality from social pathology. According to the orthodox view in philosophy,
elaborated by Hume, the 'ought' is logically separate
from the 'is' : judgements of value cannot be derived
from factual statements. For Durkheim, such a notion
separates science and practice too much. What science
can do is to discern and study the conditions of the
normal functioning of organic and of social systems,
identifying pathologies and indicating appropriate
practical measures to restore health. We can discover,
according to Durkheim, 'objective criteria, inherent in
the facts themselves' of what is normal and what is
pathological. Whether in biology or sociology, this
first of all involves a classification of species or types.
The normal blood-temperature of a lizard is different
from that of a man; what is normal for one species
is abnormal for another. Such a classification of types
of society is what Durkheim tried to work out in his
discussion of the development of the division of labour.
The point is already made there : the normal form of
morality in a simple society, dominated by mechanical

solidarity, is different from the moral order appropriate to a differentiated society cohered by organic solidarity. An approximate indication of whether a given social phenomenon is normal in a given type of society is provided by whether it is found in most or all societies that belong to that type. But this is only a preliminary criterion, for the 'normal' does not equal the 'average'. The analyst must go further, and identify the functions which the social item in question fulfils. This is especially crucial when a major process of social transformation is taking place, because new social forms will be emerging and others dropping away : we have to show by empirical study which elements are obsolete, and due to become altered or to disappear, and which are on the contrary anticipations of the needs of the emerging type.

The Division of Labour, as I have already mentioned, was designed to accomplish such an analysis for the current stage of development of the European societies. Examples drawn from that work crop up throughout *The Rules*, and it is evident how much Durkheim's thought in each study influenced the arguments developed in the other. The same is true of the third of Durkheim's major works to appear, *Suicide*. In *The Division of Labour*, Durkheim had referred to the increased suicide rates in most countries during the nineteenth century. This was a well-attested phenomenon by the time Durkheim came to the subject. A large number of statistical monographs on suicide and its causes had been published since the late eighteenth century. Many of their authors had argued that the documented rise in suicide rates throughout most of Western Europe was evidence of a moral crisis in European civilization. The so-called 'moral statisticians', among whom the Belgian demographer Quételet was a leading figure, had regarded suicide statistics, together with statistics on divorce, illegitimacy, and so on, as precise indicators of the moral state of a society.

Durkheim accepted this approach, modifying it for his own purposes, and drew heavily upon the statistical generalizations on the distribution of suicide established by previous writers. Durkheim's *Suicide* has subsequently become so well known that many authors have exaggerated the novelty of its method of statistical correlation and the results obtained. The book contains very little that was new in these respects.[4] Its unusual qualities derive more from the way in which Durkheim applied his conception of sociological method to explain suicide. Most previous authors, while acknowledging that suicide is strongly influenced by social factors, believed that causal influences such as race, or inherited mental disorder, are also important in its aetiology. In the opening part of his book, Durkheim set out to show this was not the case. Comparing the distribution of suicide with that of 'non-social' factors, he concluded that none of the latter can explain the observed differences in suicide rates : we must look for an exclusively sociological explanation.

Suicide, in other words, is a social fact, and has to be explained by means of other social facts. To be more accurate : the task of sociology in the explanation of suicide is not to account for all its aspects, certain of which it is the business of psychology to study; suicide is a social fact only in terms of its social distribution. The sociologist has to consider suicide, not as an aggregate of individual acts, but as a patterned phenomenon. If 'the suicides committed in a given society during a given period of time are taken as a whole,' we find that 'this total is not simply a sum of independent units, a collective total, but is itself a new fact *sui generis*, with its own unity, individuality, and consequently its own nature.'[5] The suicide rate remains fairly stable in any given society from year to year (although occasionally there are sharp flunctuations and there are long-term trends that may be discerned in it). This stability affirms, according to Durkheim, that we are in the presence of a social fact. For we can be certain that the individuals who figure in the suicide rate in one year are not the same as those who compose it the next; there must be certain social influences which are acting upon all these individuals.

If we compare the suicide rates of the European countries, Durkheim pointed out, we find marked, and stable, differences between them. The suicide rate for England, for example, is twice as high as that of Italy; that of Denmark is four times as high as the English rate. It is not difficult to see (and many others before Durkheim had noted) that suicide rates are lowest in the Catholic countries, and are at their peak in the Protestant ones. Those societies in which there are mixed populations of Catholics and Protestants tend to have rates in between these extremes. How are we to account for this influence of religious denomination upon the distribution of suicide? We cannot do so, Durkheim thought, in terms of the character of beliefs prohibiting suicide. Suicide is condemned with equal severity by both Catholic and Protestant dogma. The most important difference between Catholicism and Protestantism is the spirit of free enquiry which the latter permits, and indeed enjoins upon those within the religious community. The Protestant is alone before

43

God; in Catholicism, on the other hand, the priesthood intervenes between the believer and the deity, according to a traditionally ordered system of beliefs and practices. The Catholic Church, in short, is a 'more strongly integrated' social community than the Protestant, and it is from this difference that the divergences in suicide rates derive. Such an explanation also shows why England has a lower suicide rate than other predominantly Protestant societies: the Anglican Church retains a priestly hierarchy and traditional forms of worship.

This establishes a causal generalization linking social solidarity and suicide. The suicide rate of a religious community is inversely related to the level of social integration of that community: the more strongly integrated the religious society, the lower its rate of suicide. This leads us to suspect that the connection between social integration and suicide can be extended. The suicide rates of unmarried people are generally higher than those of married persons of comparable age. Marriage may, as is commonly assumed, involve burdens and responsibilities of which the single person is free, yet it has a protecting influence against suicide insofar as it integrates the individual into a stable social relationship. This is confirmed, Durkheim argued, by the inverse relation between suicide and size of the family unit: the more children in the family, the lower the rate of the parents' suicide. We can thus develop a second generalization, namely, that suicide is inversely related to the degree of social integration of domestic society; for a large family tends to be a more closely-structured group, involving more binding social ties, than a small family or a marital pair alone. Since this relation between suicide and social solidarity holds regardless of the institution involved, the connection can be stated at the most abstract level as the following proposition: 'suicide varies inversely with the degree of integration of the social groups of which the individual forms a part.' (P. 209.) This is a distinctive type of suicide: 'egoistic suicide'.

Egoistic suicide is only one form of suicide found in contemporary society. A second type is linked to that condition of the moral order which Durkheim referred to in *The Division of Labour* as 'anomie'. In that work, the cyclical tendency of the modern economy is treated as one expression of the deregulated state of industry. In *Suicide* Durkheim showed a correlation between the fluctuations of the economy and suicide: suicide rates rise quite steeply in times of economic depression. This cannot be due simply to material poverty, Durkheim reasoned, because those who have always been poor in fact usually show low rates of suicide. Moreover, suicide rates do not only increase during depressions: they rise to an equivalent degree when there is a marked period of economic boom. Hence the causative factor is not the material circumstances themselves, but the instability which they introduce into social life. In circumstances of social disruption, the moral codes that customarily regulate individuals' social activities are placed under strain, and tend to lose their hold.

Economic fluctuation is not the only cause of anomic suicide. The deregulated condition of the division of labour, Durkheim argued, also provides a more chronic source of the same type of suicide. Suicide is much more frequent among those working in commerce and industry than among those working in agricultural

45

occupations. Within the former spheres, suicide rates are directly related to socio-economic status: those at the highest levels have the highest rates of suicide. This cannot be explained, Durkheim pointed out, from the premises of utilitarianism, according to which happiness is facilitated by reward, such that the greater the rewards an individual achieves the more content he is with his existence. What has happened in the modern period is that needs and desires have become freed from moral constraint, so that they have lost any fixed point of reference. In previous times, a traditional moral order (which still maintains a greater hold in rural areas than in commercial-industrial settings) adjusted expectations to income. Its influence 'was felt by workers and masters, the poor and the rich. It consoled the former and taught them contentment with their lot by informing them of the providential nature of the social order, that the share of each class was assigned by God himself, and by holding out the hope for just compensation in a world to come in return for the inequalities of this world.' (P. 254.) This traditional moral order has eroded with the growth of the modern division of labour, while the new forms of moral control of economic life have still to become well established. The consequence is that desires become unmoderated. The quest to make more and more money is unlimited, and therefore unrealizable; however successful an individual is in accumulating wealth he may still feel unfulfilled. Since this empty space of unbounded aspiration is nearer to those at the top levels of the economic system, they are more prone to suicide than others in less elevated positions.

It must be acknowledged that the differences between egoistic and anomic suicide, as set out by Durkheim, are not always clear. Since society is the source of moral regulation, one might suppose that individuals who are inadequately integrated into social communities thereby find themselves in a situation of anomie. At several points in *Suicide*, Durkheim admitted that the social origins of the two overlap. Even so, the general connections between egoistic and anomic suicide and the analysis of social development worked out in *The Division of Labour* are evident enough. Each of these types of suicide is the product of the social changes which undermine mechanical solidarity. Egoistic suicide seems to some extent an unavoidable offshoot of the rise of moral individualism since, as Durkheim put it, while 'individualism is of course not necessarily egoism . . . it comes close to it; the one cannot be stimulated without the other being enlarged.' (P. 364.) Anomic suicide, by contrast, is largely the outcome of the transitional state of the contemporary socio-economic order: it will decline, although, according to Durkheim, not disappear altogether, with the remoralization of the industrial system.

In the first edition of *The Division of Labour*, Durkheim wrote that suicide is 'extremely rare' in traditional societies. He changed his mind about this later, and in subsequent editions of the book the statement was omitted. He was, however, already convinced that suicide in the simpler societies is distinct from that in the more advanced, and tried to document this at some length in *Suicide*. If in modern society people kill themselves because life is meaningless, in traditional society they do so because death is meaningful: values exist which make self-destruction, for certain categories of individuals, an honourable or even an obligatory act. For instance, in some societies, it is the duty of a wife to put herself to death on the demise of her husband; in others, those who become infirm must commit suicide rather than be a burden upon the community. Durkheim's term for this type of suicide is 'altruistic suicide', and it is counterposed to egoistic suicide: in the first, the integration of the individual into the social community, and respect for its values, is the source of the suicidal act, whereas the second derives precisely from the absence of such integrative ties.

3 The State and Politics

The terms 'mechanical' and 'organic solidarity', omni-present in *The Division of Labour*, rarely appear in Durkheim's later writings. Throughout his intellectual career he remained committed to the fundamental views expressed in that work, but at the same time became dissatisfied with some aspects of his early formulation of the contrast between the two major types of social solidarity. The dominant themes of his later work, in his lecture courses and in his published writings, may aptly be seen as directed to amending and expanding upon the implications of the typology. His developing concern with religion culminated in *The Elementary Forms*, which is effectively a reworked theory of mechanical solidarity. So far as contemporary society is concerned, the discussion of organic solidarity in *The Division of Labour* was elaborated into a detailed analysis of the social changes demanded in the modern era, of the challenge presented by socialism, and of the nature of modern politics.

According to Marcel Mauss, Durkheim early on decided to devote his doctoral dissertation to a study of 'the relationship of individualism and socialism'.[1] This is not what the book eventually became, although some of its ideas were influenced by those of the reformist socialists or the so-called 'academic socialists' in Germany, with whose work Durkheim had become acquainted in his year of study there. His lecture course on socialism was thus the first place in which he con-

fronted socialist doctrines in a direct way. It deals with
the origins of modern socialism and with Saint-Simon.
Unfortunately that was as far as Durkheim ever got.
The second part of the lecture course, in which he
planned to cover, among other thinkers, Lassalle, Marx
and Engels, never materialized, partly because he turned
his energies towards organizing the *Année Sociologique*.
Nevertheless, there is sufficient material in the socialism
lectures to make it possible to identify the essentials
of his attitude towards Marxism.

Durkheim began his course by introducing a distinction between 'socialism' and 'communism'. Socialism is a product of the social changes which have
occurred in European societies since the eighteenth
century. The main impetus to the rise of socialist
theories is a perception of the chaotic state of modern
economic life, which has broken away from traditional
modes of production and in the process has created
economic forces that dominate men more than men
dominate them. The remedy for this, proposed by
socialist thinkers, is to bring these economic forces
back under control by centralizing the economy in
the hands of directive institutions. Socialists 'demand
the linking of commercial and industrial activities to
the directing and conscious agencies of society.' (P. 54.)
Of course, different socialist theories provide differing
versions of how this is to be accomplished, and what
the resulting society will look like. But it is important
to Durkheim's discussion, and to his analysis of the
limitations of socialist ideas, that socialism is essentially a body of economic doctrines. This, for him, was
expressed most clearly in Saint-Simon's famous idea
that in the society of the future the administration of
people is to be replaced by the administration of things.

For while several types of socialism see the state as
the agency which will, by conscious direction, over-
come the irrationalities of modern economic life, at
the same time they regard the state, as it now exists,
as an institution to be transcended. As Saint-Simon
held, this is possible because the role of the state is
to become purely economic; political domination is to
be something of the past. For this reason, we cannot
treat most forms of anarchism as wholly separate from
socialism. The theme that political power is to be
replaced by economic administration also appears in
the former, save that the directive agencies are conceived of as being decentralized. Durkheim emphasized
that it is not a trait of socialism to require the subordination of economic activities to the state: rather,
economic functions are to replace political ones.

'Socialism' and 'communism', Durkheim pointed out,
were often used as equivalent and interchangeable
terms in the literature of political theory. But it is
essential to distinguish the two – even if their influence
can become commingled. For communism is not, as
socialism is, a creation of a specific time and place.
Communist ideas, which develop utopias, appear
sporadically over the course of history, from Classical
to modern times. The term 'socialism', in contrast to
'communism', is relatively new, having come into use
only in the early years of the nineteenth century.
Communist ideas are normally fashioned by individual
authors, as detailed blueprints of just forms of society.
The works of Plato, More and Campanella are the most
prominent examples. Communist theories, according
to Durkheim, express the personalities of particular
thinkers more than they reflect social conditions. 'They
are dreams in which generous spirits take delight,

which draw attention and maintain interest because of their nobility and dignity, but which, not answering the real needs felt by the social organism, exist in the imagination and remain practically unproductive.' (P. 66.) These characteristics are exemplified by the very nature of utopian writings, which normally place their ideal society in a fictional setting.

Two further features of communism distinguished by Durkheim are worth mentioning. One is that communist theories are essentially moral doctrines, which identify private property or wealth as the origin of most human evils: private wealth releases impulses for self-aggrandisement that bring human beings into conflict with one another. Second, as a result of this, communist theory holds that the economic and political spheres have to be kept strictly separate: those who are charged with political authority must not be exposed to the corruption which follows the desire for wealth. This is an evident characteristic of Plato's *Republic*, which is the original model inspiring most subsequent visions of utopia. In Plato's society, the inferior classes of labourers and artisans have no rights of political participation, and are excluded from military service. The political and military leaders, on the other hand, are denied access to private property, and must live a frugal, communal life. In communist theory, Durkheim stated, consumption is communal and production private; the opposite is true of socialist theory. Communism is based upon fear of the corrupting influence of wealth; socialism upon the impulsion to expand the realm of industrial production to create more wealth for all.

For Durkheim, it is as important to distinguish socialism from communism as it is to separate mechan-

ical and organic solidarity – and for the same reasons.
The transitional state of development in which the
European societies find themselves makes it essential
to sort out what belongs to the past from that which is
a legitimate anticipation of the future. In existing
political doctrines (including Marxism), elements from
communism and socialism are frequently mixed together. Many thinkers have failed clearly to differenti-
ate one from the other because, although the social
reforms they imply are different and even mutually
opposed, they each share a concern with the deleterious
consequences which the pursuit of private interests
has for the welfare of the community as a whole. But
separate them we must. Communism is not an early
form of socialism. The reason why Durkheim thought
it was not is easy enough to trace, in the light of the
thesis of *The Division of Labour*. Indeed, at one point
in the socialism lectures it is made explicit. Communist
theories relate to the conditions of a society with only
a rudimentary division of labour. In utopia, production
is a private matter. Everyone labours at similar tasks,
but as independent producers. Production is not a
co-operative enterprise, bringing a diversity of workers
together in a single (but internally differentiated)
economic system: the latter is only created by the
expansion of the division of labour. The difference
between the type of society presupposed in communism, and that which is presumed in socialist theories

is as great as that which separates the organization of
certain colonies of polyps from that of the higher
animals. In the first, each of the associated individuals
hunts on his own account; but what he catches is placed
in a community store. He does not own what he con-

tributes; that is to say, he cannot eat without all society eating at the same time. By contrast, among vertebrates each organ of the body functions according to rules which harmonize its relations with others . . . the distance is no less great between the two social conceptions which have so frequently been seen as similar to one another. (P. 71.)

Socialism, unlike communism, is thus an expression of the social changes produced by a complex division of labour. It does not follow that it is an accurate representation of them. Socialist theories are extremely significant in the context of the contemporary world, because socialist thinkers have grasped the fact that society is undergoing a major process of transformation, demanding new forms of regulation and direction of social life. Socialism, however, is not a science, even if, since Marx, it has become linked to claims to scientific reputability. Socialism is above all a practical programme, a call to action, and as such goes beyond what can be legitimately said to be empirically established truths about society. Durkheim acknowledged Marx's *Capital* to be the central work in recent socialist thought, 'the most systematic, the richest in ideas'. But it broaches issues that demand investigation far more exhaustive than any one person could achieve. Socialist theories are as much symptoms of the crisis they diagnose as they are the remedy: socialism is 'a cry of grief, sometimes of anger, uttered by men who feel most keenly our collective *malaise*'. (P. 41.)

Durkheim had three main criticisms of socialist ideas, as he characterized them. One is that socialism supposes that the type of regulation needed by the emerging society can be purely economic. For Durkheim, this showed that socialist doctrines are tied to views of which they were nominally in antithesis: those of utilitarianism and classical political economy. The socialists recognize that the reduction of society to economic relations of contract produces massive social dislocation; but they substitute for this only a stress upon the conscious direction of economic life. Both schools of thought fail to see that economic change must be accompanied by the development of moral regulation.

Second, socialist theories anticipate the transcendence of the state and political power: as a coordinating centre for the administration of society, the state will lose its separate identity, and become one institution among others in civil society. Durkheim disclaimed that this idea was either feasible or desirable – for reasons discussed in chapter 3.

Third, and of basic importance, Durkheim rejected the thesis that the realization of socialism involves class struggle. Socialism pertains to the need for economic regulation. Other concerns are either inspired by a misplaced communism, or are secondary to that need. 'The improvement of the workers' lot', Durkheim remarked, 'is . . . not a special objective; it is but one of the consequences that the attachment of economic activities to the managing agents of society must produce.' (P. 60.) This comment was directed against Marxist theory and, so far as it goes, is accurate enough. But it ignores some of the major claims of Marxism: in particular, those that the capitalist division of labour is a system of power, in which the only medium of change is the active struggles of the subordinate class; and that economic regulation can produce a just and equitable society only if the major institutions of society (including the division of labour itself) are thoroughly transformed.[2] For Durkheim, the necessary changes were to come about by a process of social evolution, assisted by the intervention of a beneficent state.

Durkheim's interpretation of the modern polity is found mainly in a series of lectures which he gave first in Bordeaux over a period of ten years and, later, in modified form, at the Sorbonne (*Professional Ethics and Civic Morals*), and in his preface to the second edition of *The Division of Labour*. In the lectures, Durkheim offered a developed theory of the state and its relation to contemporary politics. The conception of the state is brought closely in line with the general character of his approach. Neither of the ideas that figure so prominently in Max Weber's famous definition of the state – the claim to a legitimate monopoly over the instruments of violence, and the reference to a fixed territorial area – are part of Durkheim's concept.[3] The existence of territorial boundaries is specifically rejected as a necessary criterion for the existence of the state. Territoriality is, according to Durkheim, a relatively recent phenomenon, connected with factors other than the state itself; some nomad societies have possessed a differentiated political apparatus. Two other characteristics are accepted as relevant to the concept of the state, without being sufficient criteria. One is the existence of an authority division, separating those who command from those who obey. Where this appears, we can speak of a 'political society'. Not all societies in history are political societies, in this sense; conversely, not all groups which display this division are whole societies. The most simple societies lack a differentiated system of administrative authority. On the other hand, we find institutions within societies which have a governmental system in miniature: as in the case of the Roman patriarchal family, ruled by a head and a family council. A second characteristic, which can be appealed to so as to exclude examples of this sort, is that the population subject to the authority of the state should be numerically large. This is not a satisfactory criterion thus formulated, according to Durkheim, but it can be expressed more accurately in a different way: namely, that a political society is not a single kinship unit, but implies the existence of multiple kinship groups and other associations. We can define a political society in terms of these two attributes, as a society 'formed by the coming together of a rather large number of secondary social groups, subject to the same one authority which is not itself subject to any other authority duly constituted'.[4] The state can then be regarded as the organization of officials who are entrusted with the administration of governmental authority in a political society.

We may distinguish three accounts of the relation between the state, society and the individual from which Durkheim tried to distance his own theory. The first is that which he identified with Hegel's political philosophy, among others. In this view, according to Durkheim, the state is elevated above society, and the individual member of society is treated only as an instrument for the realization of the state's ambitions. This is essentially a conservative theory, Durkheim pointed out, and is a pathological condition of the polity if concretely found in an advanced society — as, in his pamphlet on German militarism, written during the First World War, he argued, had in fact happened in Germany.[5] The other two theories I have mentioned previously : those associated with utilitarianism and socialism. In contrast to the first type of view, each of these is basically hostile to the state as a political authority, although their versions of what should be its proper role differ. For the utilitarians and political economists, the scope of state authority should be limited to the protection of contracts, leaving everything else open to the free play of market forces. Here it is held that 'the prerogatives of the state should be limited to the administration of a wholly negative justice'. (P. 52.) The socialists wish to extend the scope of the state in one direction, in respect of the control of economic life; but socialist theory also anticipates the transcendence of the political character of the state. For them, the state will become merged with society.

In Durkheim's view, not only must the state retain important moral functions in a developed society, but its role has to become extended. The progressive emergence of the state as an institution differentiated from the institutions of civil society is a normal outcome of the growth of the division of labour, and is not a trend which can be reversed. The idea that the division between state and society can be eliminated, and political power thereby transcended, presupposes a movement back to a form of society which is now obsolete. It is only in the least advanced type of social order, which is not yet sufficiently differentiated internally to have become a political society, that there can be no state. It is mistaken to regard such a society as a democracy, because in fact its individual members have very little freedom : each is dominated by the *conscience collective*, subject to the 'tyranny of the group'. The development of the division of labour, as Durkheim had already made clear in the work of that title, is the condition of the expansion of human liberties. At first sight, as he recognized, there appears to be something of a contradiction here. For it might be presumed that the extension of the role of the state necessarily encroaches upon the freedom of the individual. According to him, however, it does not. Precisely the opposite: the state is charged with the task of concretely helping to actualize the ideals of moral individualism. 'Our moral individuality, far from being antagonistic to the state, has on the contrary been the product of it.' (P. 68.) This is not to say that he failed to recognize that, under some circumstances, the state can threaten individual freedoms. In identifying these circumstances, he worked out a distinctive theory of democracy, in the context of an advocacy of the creation of 'occupational associations' or *corporations*.

Several ideas traditionally associated with notions of democracy are rejected. A democracy, as follows from the arguments mentioned so far, is not to be identified with a society in which the state is weak. Nor, Durkheim went on to add, is a democracy a society in which everyone in some way participates directly in the enactment of authoritative decisions. In a complex, advanced society, government is necessarily in the hands of a minority. The conditions of a democratic order thus have to concern the nature of the connections between the state and society. The state, in Durkheim's eyes, is an instrument of decision-making which focuses and co-ordinates the policies relating to the needs of the individuals in civil society. The state is an 'organ of consciousness', whose role is to summarize but also to go beyond the diffuse ideas and sentiments of the population as a whole. The state has to be responsive to the views of the citizenry, but has the responsibility of articulating these clearly and rationally, discerning their implications and formulating relevant policies. A democratic society is one in which the state is independent and strong enough to accomplish these tasks, but is nevertheless in close communication with the ideas of the mass of the population. A democracy is a 'political system by which the society can achieve a consciousness of itself in its purest form. The more that deliberation and reflection and a critical spirit play a considerable part in the course of public affairs, the more democratic the nation. It is the less democratic to the degree that lack of consciousness, uncharted customs, obscure sentiments and prejudices that escape enquiry, predominate.' (P. 89.) In societies where the state is weak, the result is either the manifest dominance of custom and habit or – what really comes to the same thing – a flurry of superficial change masking a deep conservatism and resistance to innovation. The latter was effectively Durkheim's characterization of the situation of nineteenth-century France. Societies which are 'stormy on the surface', he wrote, 'are often bound to routine.' (P. 94.)

If a democratic polity does not necessarily imply the strict limitation of the influence of the state, how is the individual in civil society to be protected against an indefinite extension of state control over social and economic life? This is where secondary groups, especially the *corporations*, are due to play a major part in the political order of contemporary society. The state may become tyrannical if it is not counterbalanced by the existence of social associations which intervene between it and the individual. Such secondary groups, as Durkheim envisaged them, are to have a dual role: they should provide a buffer (as well as a mutual connection) between the state and the individual, shielding him from its possible excesses; but they have also to help to maintain the distance between civil society and the state necessary to ensure that the social order does not lapse into the conservatism of un-reflective routine.

It is not difficult to see how Durkheim's analysis of the *corporations* forms a part of the reworked theory of organic solidarity. In *The Division of Labour*, Durkheim made it clear that the new ideas of moral individualism lack the binding power exerted by the more encompassing type of traditional moral order over social conduct. He was committed to the notion that a society with a differentiated division of labour could not revert to this traditional type of moral framework, but neither on the other hand could it become as the utilitarians portrayed it, a society based on self-interest organized through contractual exchange. While these ideas were well developed in the book, the work did not really provide a convincing interpretation either of how the 'non-contractual element in contract' was to be effectively ordered, or of how the ideals of moral individualism were to be practically sustained and furthered. Durkheim's account of the role of the state helped to provide an answer to the second of these problems, but this could not in and of itself resolve the first. For, as Durkheim stressed in *The Division of Labour*, the progress of social differentiation is also one of moral differentiation. Moral individualism provides a general consensual system relating to the overall order, but cannot directly moralize different occupational tasks, for these obviously involve specialized codes which refer to the specific type of activity involved. This is to be the task the *corporations* are to accomplish.

According to Durkheim's analysis, the creation of these corporate groups may be expected to come about as part of the 'normal' process of development of the division of labour. Occupational groups were a prominent feature of the medieval economy. The medieval *corporations* or guilds united members of the same occupation within a fraternal and solidary group, providing moral rules which specified the rights and obligations of workers and employers. The old *corporations* have been destroyed by the development of large-scale commerce and industry, and we cannot presume that they will re-emerge in the same form. But their very existence shows that it is a characteristic of the division of labour to moralize occupational life. The trade unions, as they are currently organized, do not fulfil this function. They represent the beginnings of occupational organization, but they operate only as conflict-groups rather than as moral communities. Perhaps the example closest to what Durkheim expected would come into being at all levels of the occupational system are modern professional associations, which specify the moral codes that their members are required to observe in their dealings with each other and with their clients. Durkheim envisaged that the occupational groups would come to play a major role in political life in modern society, as well as having other responsibilities towards their members. The *corporations* would function as intermediary electoral colleges, replacing the direct franchise: this would be an essential element of their mediation between the individual and the state.

4 Moral Authority and Education

Durkheim began his intellectual career with the attempt to found a 'science of morality'. This endeavour led him to sociology, which was to provide the method for such a science. But the formulation of that method in turn led him back to morality, since the moral character of social facts is their distinguishing feature. Durkheim thus returned to problems of morality and ethics in his later career, as he did to philosophical questions more generally. As he wrote in a letter to Davy: 'Having begun from philosophy, I tend to return to it; or rather I have been quite naturally brought back to it by the nature of the questions which I met with en route.'[1] In the earlier part of his work, he apparently felt no inclination or need to confront moral philosophy philosophically: rather, he sought to show that sociological method, applied in a comparative way, could illuminate traditional philosophical problems. In his first writings, up to and including *The Division of Labour*, Durkheim seems to have presumed that we can only characterize morality by a process of inductive discovery. That is to say, he held that the first premise of any comprehensive discussion of moral life is that we should study diverse types of moral conduct, in the context of differing forms of society. We cannot 'legislate' what is and what is not moral activity without first studying the variability of moral codes, and determining the social conditions to which they are functionally related.

This might be taken to imply that we cannot have a universal theory of morality – a theory of morality that will hold in every type of society – since what counts as moral conduct is determined purely by the functional exigencies of societies, and societies differ in terms of such functional exigencies. Probably Durkheim never held such a view, which would imply not just a cultural, but a moral relativism.[2] It is quite consistent with his ideas to suppose that, by the middle part of his career, he believed he had succeeded in ascertaining that there are general conditions of social existence which underline the major differences in codes of moral conduct observed in varying societies. He was certainly assisted in reaching this conclusion by the new appreciation of the significance of religion which, as I have mentioned before, derived from his encounter with contemporary anthropological writings on that subject. As well as initiating the studies which culminated in *The Elementary Forms*, these stimulated him to attempt a systematic treatment of problems of morality, on a philosophical as well as a sociological level.

In these discussions (most readily available in the books published posthumously under the titles *Moral Education* and *Sociology and Philosophy*), Durkheim expanded upon points introduced in his previous works, elaborating upon them and drawing out their general implications. He had been early on impressed by Kant's insistence upon the imperative, or obligatory, character of moral rules, and this was one of the sources of his identification of the constraining character of social facts in *The Rules*. As I have indicated earlier (pp. 36-7), he had not originally separated clearly enough the features of specifically moral sanctions which dis-

moral conduct. But if this is the case, it follows that the same is true of acts directed towards others as of self-interested behaviour. If the individual in furthering his own interests does not engage in moral action, the same must be true of conduct oriented to the interests of others. This is not to say, Durkheim hastened to add, that acts directed towards others can have no moral content; everyday experience shows that the reverse is the case. What it does make clear is that the nature of moral conduct cannot be explicated in terms of individual interests, whether those of the self or of others. Morality derives from a source which goes beyond individual interests, although it may become transferred to them:

> If we cannot be bound my duty to conscious beings and we have eliminated the individual, there remains as the only other possible object of moral activity the *sui generis* collective being founded by the plurality of individuals associated to form a group . . . We arrive then at the conclusion that . . . society is a moral being qualitatively different from the individuals it comprises and from the aggregation from which it derives. (P. 51.)

This thesis, Durkheim declared, is similar to Kant's argument for the existence of God: we must hypothesise God's existence, since without that the notion of morality can have no sense. In place of God in this theorem, we put society; as Durkheim was to try to show in *The Elementary Forms*, society is indeed the very source of the idea of God itself. The common view that morality begins with disinterestedness thus contains an essential kernel of truth. Disinterest, however, connotes an affiliation to an object which surpasses individual interests. 'Between God and society', Durkheim wrote rhetorically, 'lies the choice' – not, of course, a choice at all if God is in any case only a transfigured representation of society.

The notion of authority, Durkheim stressed, is integral to morality. Moral codes are not merely customary forms of behaviour. Authority is in turn closely related to discipline. We do not apply the term 'moral' to activity which only occurs sporadically or intermittently. The notion of morality implies regularity of conduct; discipline ensures such regularity of behaviour. Discipline is not merely a means to moral ends: it is good in itself. To show why this is so brings us back to the issue of egoism. The main core of moral obligations, according to Durkheim's argument, are those which apply to the routine demands of day-to-day existence. 'Duties are not fulfilled intermittently in a blaze of glory.'[4] Such a state of affairs can only be realized through the internal control of behaviour, not through the imposition of external sanctions alone. Discipline, or more specifically self-discipline, is moral in itself because it is the medium whereby egoistic impulses are subordinated. Many moral philosophers, especially the utilitarians, have supposed that discipline and freedom of action are antithetical. But the absence of moral discipline equals anomie: moral codes provide the necessary framework for an autonomous and satisfying human existence. Socially created aspirations and interests need socially defined horizons to limit them, or the result is insatiable egoism. This is not the path to self-fulfilment, but to world-weariness.

It is not difficult to see how this view of morality leads to the conclusion that man is a *homo duplex*, the creature of dual sets of motives, insofar as egoism and moral conduct are discrete and in chronic potential opposition. Durkheim did draw just this conclusion, and also established a connection between it and certain sorts of religious beliefs. 'In every age', he wrote, 'man has been intensely aware of this duality. He has, in fact, everywhere conceived of himself as being formed of two radically heterogeneous beings: the body and the soul . . . not only are these two beings substantially different, they are in a large measure independent of each other, and are often even in conflict.'[5] Body and soul exist as one, but they belong to different realms of existence; the soul is a sacred force, inhabiting the profane object which is the body. This symbolic dualism is an expression of the real tension between two sides of the human personality, sensations and sensory needs on the one hand, conceptual thought and moral activity on the other. Needs such as hunger or thirst are the prototype of egoistic drives, because they relate only to the self, although any motive dominated by self-concern comes within this category. Morality on the other hand, as disinterested activity, is oriented to impersonal principles that can be universalized. All moral acts, even those most dominated by enthusiasm, involve some element of constraint, some degree of self-sacrifice. Man is necessarily a 'mixed and contradictory being'.

This has all the makings of a potentially reactionary doctrine, as in some respects it definitely is. There is no dearth of commentators on Durkheim's writings, both hostile and sympathetic, who have treated his theory of moral authority as expressing a straightforwardly conservative standpoint. But this is misleading, if not simply mistaken, unless one wishes to understand by 'conservative' everything which is not revolutionary. Durkheim quite clearly intended his general account of morality to be both compatible with, and read in the light of, the transformation of moral standards that has been brought about by the transition from mechanical to organic solidarity. We might not accept that his views always are internally consistent with one another; nonetheless, the main outline of how he wished to connect up his abstract account of moral conduct with his interpretation of social change is evident. A concrete exemplification of his ideas in these respects is provided by his writings on education, which I shall refer to briefly at the end of this chapter.

Discipline is an essential aspect of moral conduct, Durkheim held, but its character changes in the course of social evolution. Human freedom cannot be analysed outside of history, as philosophers have traditionally believed, because it is the product of social transformation. There is more than one sense in which society extends our freedoms, but all depend upon the transmutation of human faculties through membership of society, and their elevation above the merely adaptive, immediate existence of the animals. One dimension in which society has a liberating effect is in freeing man from subjection to the world of nature, in delivering him 'from blind unthinking physical forces'.[6] His submission to society is the condition of this liberation. In the most simple forms of society, this submission is more or less total. The level of individuality and autonomy of action are low. In these societies, 'the simplicity of moral behaviour makes it easy to transform such behaviour into habits, mechanically carried out . . . custom and tradition have such power and prestige as to leave no place for reasoning and question-

ing'. Moral discipline is taken for granted as traditionally given; it does not have to acquire a rational basis.
The latter is demanded, however, as society becomes
more complex; moral codes can no longer be sustained
unreflectively, so as to go beyond the scope of considered judgement. 'It does not follow from a belief
in discipline', Durkheim asserted, 'that discipline must
involve blind and slavish submission.' In a differentiated
society, dominated by the ideals of moral individualism,
conformity must 'not amount to passive resignation,
but to enlightened allegiance'.[7]

The formal educational system, Durkheim believed,
has to play a vital role in the inculcation of the moral
attitudes and capacities required in a society oriented
towards these secular ideals. In his lectures on peda-
gogy, he did not restrict the term 'education' to the
sense of formal instruction, using it in a sense closer
to that which 'socialization' has come to have in
English, since he wanted to undertake a study of
moral and intellectual development at different
stages of evolution. 'Education', according to Durkheim's definition, 'is the influence exercised by adult
generations on those that are not yet ready for
social life.'[8] In accordance with his characteristic
views on moral philosophy generally, Durkheim stressed
that it is fruitless to attempt to formulate abstract
educational values; differing educational systems are
directed to differing ideals, according to the type of
society in which they are found. Education varies
between different strata within society: in types of
society prior to modern times, literary and other
educational arts have been the prerogative of small
elite groups. Today, Durkheim added, there still are
major differences between the classes in terms of the

character and level of the formal education typically enjoyed. These latter differences, however, he affirmed, reiterating the thesis of *The Division of Labour*, are due to disappear: the education children receive must no longer be determined by the class position into which they happen to be born. On the other hand, occupational specialization is an intrinsic characteristic of present-day society, and since different occupations demand the development of specialized knowledge, the modern educational system, once the child gets beyond a certain age, has to be vocational. This heterogeneity will no longer rest upon 'unjust inequalities', but has to be reflected in the diversification of the system of education. But however specialized particular forms of education may become, there will remain a shared core of educational experience. This will apply in the future, and has always been the case in the past. Even in the Indian caste system, with its rigid definition of strata, there were beliefs which everyone learned to accept, gods which everyone had to acknowledge. Since modern morality is becoming secular, the theistic content of education has to disappear: the modern educational system must transmit secular values and codes of conduct which permit the autonomy of action called for by the differentiated division of labour.

In France in the late nineteenth century, the role of the state in education was still a matter of controversy, and the struggle to achieve secular control of education protracted. Durkheim stated bluntly where his sympathies lay, and what he believed his analysis of morality and education showed to be necessary. Those who advocate that responsibility for education should be primarily the prerogative of the family or the Church, or a combination of the two, are out of tune with the demands of the modern social order. They hold that the part played by the state should be kept at a minimum. But the state is a crucial moral agency in contemporary society, and thus cannot stand aloof from the educational system. The state has to assume general direction of the school syllabus, guaranteeing that the latter reflects the ideals to which society is dedicated, and also ensuring that children are educated for the roles they will have to assume in the specialised division of labour. Durkheim accepted that the state should tolerate the continuation of schools which it does not itself directly administer: but it should nonetheless have the power to oversee the curriculum of such schools.

Durkheim's education lectures (*Moral Education*) contain a lengthy discussion of the sociology of the modern school and the responsibilities of the teacher. In these lectures, the nature of school discipline and its relation to the exigencies of moral discipline more generally, are at the centre of Durkheim's concerns. The behaviour of the young child is dominated by the unstable impulses of egoism; young children display rapid fluctuation of attention and emotion, a spirit which does not sit easily with the regularity of conduct required by moral discipline. Education thus must involve 'the moderation of desires and self-mastery', although these qualities can only be acquired as part of a gradual process. According to Durkheim, the immediate and volatile character of children's behaviour closely resembles that of the adult members of the simpler societies. Thus the educational process in an advanced society recapitulates the elements of the development of civilization as a whole. This is not merely a matter of encouraging tendencies which are

73

latent in the child since, as has been made clear in the general analysis of moral conduct, moral behaviour always involves some constraint against which the egoistic inclinations of the individual may chafe. The moral education of the child has to make use of two features of his nature: the strong influence which habit tends to acquire in children's behaviour, and the effects which can be wielded through the implementation of adult authority. Habit can become moulded into moral discipline. But the teacher must also establish himself as a moral exemplar, who conditions the child's behaviour through his demeanour as well as through direct instruction.

The two forms of moral sanction, positive and negative, appear in Durkheim's sociology of education in relation to the use of reward and punishment within the school. The inculcation of discipline in schools is often associated with physical as well as other forms of punishment that may be inflicted upon the wayward child. How strong should be the social discipline of the classroom, and should schools in the future retain corporal punishment? Durkheim's portrayal of the character that the classroom atmosphere should take is a dour one. The qualities of moral autonomy which the modern school system has to help to produce are not to be learned through play or free self-expression. The child 'must be introduced to the sober things of life'. On the other hand, we should recognize that 'social life is not military life'. Moral codes have to be accepted as desirable and attractive as well as demanding restraint: 'respect for discipline does not originate in the fear of sanctions curbing violations of the rule.'[9] A school in which punishment is frequently and harshly applied is precisely one in which the authorities have lost the moral respect necessary for discipline. One theory of punishment offered by some educators holds that a child must be punished for wrong-doing in order to prevent him from repeating his misbehaviour, and to stop others imitating him: here the function of punishment is regarded as the deterrence of misdeeds. Durkheim did not deny that such may sometimes be the case but – as the theory of repressive law developed in *The Division of Labour* indicates – did not consider deterrence to be the principal factor involved. Punishment should not be treated as merely intimidation, producing overtly correct behaviour, since such behaviour is not truly moral. The same considerations apply to punitive sanctions in the school setting as apply to repressive law in the wider society: in the school, as in the law as a whole, we must accept that punishment should fit the crime; this cannot be explained by the deterrence theory, which would logically imply that punishment should be graded according to seriousness of inclination to misconduct rather than the gravity of the misconduct itself. Punishment is a reaction to the violation of moral rules, and protects their sanctity by showing that they have lost none of their authority in the face of transgression. The teacher has to be able to wield punitive sanctions because he is the incarnation of moral authority, and by the punitive act must show his own allegiance to the values in question. This demonstrates however that it is not punishment which is the source of discipline in the school; punitive sanctions serve to defend against the undermining of that authority. What is important in educational discipline is not that the guilty party should suffer, but that he should be vigorously censured, such that he grasps and assimilates the intrinsic nature of the sanctity of moral rules. Corporal punishment thus must be prohibited in schools, Durkheim concluded. Not only does it not have the effects claimed for it by those who believe that punishment is a deterrent, it may actively contravene just those moral ideals which have become of focal importance in contemporary society: respect for the freedom and dignity of the individual, as manifest in moral individualism. 'One of the chief aims of moral education is to inspire in the child a feeling for the dignity of man. Corporal punishment is a continual offence to this sentiment.'[10]

Durkheim's account of the history of education in France (*L'Evolution pédagogique en France*) has rarely been accorded the attention it deserves in secondary discussions of his writings. It is an important work in its own right, but it also helps illuminate other aspects of Durkheim's sociology. It relies upon the perspectives developed in *The Division of Labour*, but is more concretely historical than the earlier study. The significance of history for sociological explanation, in fact, is accentuated more explicitly in *L'Evolution pédagogique* than in any other of Durkheim's major works. The theory and practice of education, Durkheim tried to show, was undergoing a process of change which reflected that being experienced by society as a whole. The French educational system was in a state of 'intellectual disarray', with strong survivals of the traditional curriculum persisting amid new developments, the introduction of the teaching of science, for instance, vying with the continuing prevalence of the classics. By undertaking an historical analysis of the evolution of educational systems, Durkheim tried to show which trends in education should be promoted, and which elements discarded.

Medieval Christianity, Durkheim claimed, has played the fundamental role in the evolution of the Western school system. In antiquity, the object of education was to permit the child to acquire a range of discrete talents: in Greece these were predominantly artistic or aesthetic, while in Rome they were more practical. But in neither was education a unified process, located in time and place, as it has since become. Medieval Christianity helped to preserve some of the emphases of Roman pagan education while integrating them within a more thorough-going emphasis upon moral discipline. Christianity fostered 'the conception that there is in each of us an underlying mode of being, from which particular forms of intelligence and sensibility derive, and in which they find their unity; and that it is this underlying mode of being which has to be reached if one wants to carry out the task of the educationalist with lasting effect . . . This result can only be obtained by making children always live in the same moral environment, the presence of which is always with them; which entirely surrounds them and the action of which, so to speak, they cannot escape. This is the explanation of the concentration of education and even the whole life of the child, with the emergence of the school as it has been organized under Christianity.'[11] In respect of education, Durkheim argued, the Middle Ages was certainly not an uninteresting, transitory period in the development of Western European culture; on the contrary, social formations were initiated whose influence has since ramified throughout our contemporary social life.

The object of education, even in a highly diversified society, is not just the training of the child in an aggregate of skills; it is at a more basic level oriented towards the creation of general dispositions of personality. In the present-day social world, this no longer can have a specifically Christian content; and the values the child learns are secular. But these values have their origin in Christian beliefs, just as the setting of the school has its beginnings in the medieval Church schools. In contemporary society, where the process of schooling becomes more and more extended, and where the family loses some of its hold over the development of the child, the unified character of the school as a social and moral environment of learning becomes even more significant.

Durkheim distinguished three major phases in the development of the theory and practice of education since the Middle Ages. In the Scholastic age, which lasted from the twelfth century until the Renaissance, most of the basic elements that constitute the modern educational system were laid down, in rudimentary form: schools, universities, faculties, degrees, and examinations. The Renaissance initiated the second phase. This stage was marked by the disintegration of Christendom as a single and coherent moral system, and the development of different educational ideals; humanistic values began to replace religious morality within the educational system. The third phase begins somewhere in the late eighteenth century, and is still in progress; here education becomes entirely secularized, and science enters in as basic to the curriculum. This shows the way which has to be further developed. According to Durkheim, Protestantism, especially Lutheranism, played an important part in the early phase of the modern period: hence the latter is more advanced in Germany than in France. The humanist stage in education was dominated by the precepts that human nature is universal and unchanging, and that the Classics are the place where it is best studied. This type of education has been important in establishing a platform for the emergence of moral individualism, but has now become outworn. The value placed upon the dignity and autonomy of the individual becomes more and more central to moral codes, but the notion that human nature is a constant has to be replaced by one which recognizes the diversity of human behaviour. The demand upon education today is to create sympathy and understanding for others, a capacity to accept change, and an awareness of the potentialities of mankind. 'Let us therefore continue the work of the humanists', Durkheim concluded, 'but by transforming it and infusing it with new ideas. Let us make use of Classical writings, not in order to allow the child to know that abstract and general concept of man which was the seventeenth-century ideal, but to show him man as he is, with his almost endless variability and with that extreme complexity of his nature which allows it to assume the most diverse forms.'[12]

5 Religion and the Theory of Knowledge

Himself a non-believer, Durkheim nevertheless had good reason to acknowledge the significance of religion in relation to moral conduct. Brought up in an orthodox Jewish milieu, he could hardly fail to feel both the influence of professed belief upon day-to-day conduct, as well as the coherence of outlook produced by a religious world-view. Whatever the influence of his own upbringing might have been on his sociological ideas, he certainly was interested in problems of the social origins and nature of religion from his very earliest writings. Among his first published articles was a lengthy review of Guyau's *L'Irréligion de l'avenir* (from which he derived the term 'anomie'). Guyau argued that religion stems from a double source: the intellectual need to understand the world around us, and the practical need of sociability. Durkheim commented that these should be put in reverse order of priority; religion has its origins in the practical demands of life in society. Men did not first invent gods, and then connect these ideas to their social activity. The cognitive formulation of religious ideas is an expression of pre-existing social sentiments which antedate their appearance in conscious reflections. One of Durkheim's articles on social thought in Germany contains a significant discussion of Wundt's theory of religion. Wundt provided, according to Durkheim, a more plausible account of the essential characteristics of religion than that of Guyau. In the simpler societies,

Wundt showed, religion is the principal source of social cohesion; religious beliefs comprise a set of 'metaphysical speculations on the nature and order of things', but these are integrated with ritual forms of conduct and moral discipline. Religion in such societies is the source of altruistic attitudes which have the effect 'of restraining egoism, of inclining man towards sacrifice and disinterestedness', thus attaching him 'to something other than himself, making him dependent upon superior powers which symbolize the ideal'.[1]

It is obvious enough how much these ideas, and comparable ones which Durkheim derived from others among his predecessors or contemporaries in the initial part of his intellectual career, influenced the views expressed in *The Division of Labour*. Most of the discussion of mechanical solidarity which Durkheim set out in that book is derivative, and it would be true to say that this was not where his main direction of interest lay (the sub-title of the book, after all, was 'a study of the organization of the developed societies'). In *The Division of Labour* it is already recognized, however, that religion is central to the beliefs and modes of conduct which cohere the less developed societies; and although there are only relatively short passages, apart from the sections on religious crimes, in which the nature of religion is analysed directly, they do contain most of the important points that were embodied within *The Elementary Forms* nineteen years later. The idea that religion can be defined as necessarily relating to supernatural beings or gods is rejected. It is suggested that religious beliefs express the character of the social totality; that religion is the original source of all forms of thought, which subsequently become secularized; and finally, that although the hold of religion over day-to-day life declines in the course of social differentiation, and the old deities disappear, the new ideals of moral individualism still preserve an intrinsically religious character.[2] But none of these themes is developed in any detail in *The Division of Labour*. Durkheim's concern was not with mechanical solidarity as such, but with its supplanting by the new mode of solidarity organized through the division of labour, and the consequences of the latter for the controversy over the fate of individualism in present-day society.

The Elementary Forms should therefore be seen as a direct continuation of the lines of thought which occupied Durkheim from the early phase of development of his work. This is not as unimportant a point as it may seem. Many of Durkheim's secondary interpreters have argued that the work culminating in *The Elementary Forms* marked a decisive shift in emphasis from his earlier writings. Thus according to Talcott Parsons's very influential study of Durkheim,[3] the latter's works can be seen as being devoted to resolving an abstract 'problem of order', deriving originally from Hobbes: what prevents society from collapsing into a struggle of each individual against every other, a 'war of all against all'? *The Division of Labour* Parsons treats as an early, and inadequate, attempt to cope with this problem; in the latter part of his career, and particularly in *The Elementary Forms*, he argues, Durkheim moved away from his earlier naturalism towards a position closer to idealism. But this interpretation does not stand up to close examination. In his very earliest writings, Durkheim held that, as he put it, 'society is the ideal', but stressed that such a view was perfectly compatible with a naturalistic approach to sociology.

He was in fact never much concerned with the 'problem of order' as defined by Parsons, asserting that Hobbes's standpoint, depending upon an argument from a state of nature, was simply irrelevant to sociology, which must transcend it.

What, then, does distinguish Durkheim's later work on religion from the ideas expressed in his earlier writings – since he admitted that he only acquired a full understanding of its significance in the middle 1890s? The question is not too difficult to answer. One reason why he found the work of the British and American anthropologists thought-provoking is simply that in their writings he for the first time encountered detailed studies of traditional societies. He did not particularly approve of the style of comparative method used by such authors as Frazer, Tylor, and Robertson-Smith – 'scissors and paste ethnology' as it later came to be called – but he found there a wealth of material, mostly concerned with religion, ritual and myth, that was far more substantial than had been available in the works of the German ethnologists upon whom he had leaned heavily when writing *The Division of Labour* and *Suicide*. Moreover, in the 1890s some of the first major field-studies of the Australian tribal societies began to appear : these Durkheim saw as providing a richer source of empirical material on the less developed societies than anything else hitherto. He reviewed Spencer and Gillen's famous study, *The Native Tribes of Central Australia* (1899), in the *Année Sociologique* in 1900, and used this very extensively in *The Elementary Forms*.

Second, on the more theoretical level, he came to appreciate more clearly than he had done before the vital importance of ritual and ceremonial in the sustaining of religious belief. In *The Division of Labour*, the origin of mechanical solidarity is left unelucidated: the continued allegiance of the members of society to the beliefs and values upon which social solidarity depends is seen as unproblematic. He later came to realize that it is not; periodic ceremonial is tightly bound up with the sustaining of such commitment. The work of Robertson-Smith seems to have played the leading part in influencing the direction of Durkheim's ideas in this respect (Robertson-Smith also regarded totemism, as Durkheim came to do, as the simplest form of religion, linked to segmentary clan societies).

Finally, Durkheim came to be more directly interested in the cognitive content of religious beliefs than he had been previously. In his own terminology, the term *représentation collective* (collective idea) came more and more to acquire precedence over *conscience collective*, the preferred term in his earlier work. In the first part of his career, he had concentrated most upon a Kantian theme, that of the moral imperative, trying to show that the origin of moral imperatives is social. If this is so on the level of morality however, we can suspect that it is also true on the level of cognition: and this is just what Durkheim went on to claim. Thus we find the emergence of a second strand of 'sociological Kantianism' in Durkheim's later writings: an endeavour to demonstrate that the basic categories of thought as identified by Kant have their origin in society.

In *The Elementary Forms* Durkheim began, as he did in all of his major works, by seeking to establish a precise definition of the phenomenon under study. Many, perhaps most, previous writers had implicitly or explicitly treated religion as essentially involving recognition of the existence of supernatural entities. But the idea of the supernatural, Durkheim declared, is actually a quite recent development, for it presupposes a certain level of secularization; the 'supernatural' only has any sense when counterposed to the 'natural world', governed by impersonal laws. Nor is the notion of a god or gods a defining characteristic of religion. One can quite easily find examples of major religions where the idea of god is absent (Durkheim cited the case of Buddhism to support this). The most distinctive characteristic of religious beliefs and symbols is the attitude with which they are approached, which severs them absolutely from the instrumental activities of ordinary daily life. All religious beliefs presuppose a polar division of reality into two opposed classes of objects: those which are 'sacred', on the one hand, and those that are 'profane' on the other. Sacred things are the subject of attitudes of awe and veneration, and thus kept completely separate from life in the profane world. Those who pass between the two realms have to undergo rituals of purification or initiation, such as is always involved when a young person reaches the age at which he is permitted to become a full member of the religious community. Those individuals who are charged with most fully exemplifying the ideals of the religious community usually have to make a complete break with the world of the profane. 'Hence comes the monasticism which is artificially organized outside of and apart from the natural environment in which the ordinary man leads the life of this world . . . Hence comes the mystic asceticism whose object is to root out from man all the attachment for the profane world that remains in him.'[4]

However, the dualism of the sacred and profane alone is not sufficient to characterize religion. Religion consists not only in beliefs, but in practices, or rituals and ceremonials. Every religion involves the existence of a 'church'. Durkheim did not use the latter term to refer to a specialized hierarchy, or priesthood, but rather to designate a regularized social organization of believers. The social practices associated with religion take place within the context of such an organization. This for Durkheim is one of the chief factors distinguishing religion from magic. Magic often involves ritual, but has no church; a magician is not the public leader of a community, but an individual with an amorphous clientele. A religion can thus be defined as 'a unified system of beliefs and practices relative to sacred things, that is to say, things apart and forbidden – beliefs and practices which unite into one single moral community called a church, all those who adhere to them.' (P. 62.)

The empirical substance upon which the arguments advanced in *The Elementary Forms* are based is taken from studies of Australian totemism, which according to Durkheim is 'the most primitive and simple form of religion known to us today'. (P. 13.) The notion of evolutionary differentiation upon which Durkheim relied in his work meant he had no particular qualms in holding that the simplest form of religion must be found in the simplest type of society. In the most simple type of society we can observe religion in its most 'elementary form'; that is to say, we can find the most basic elements of religious life, that underlie the more differentiated kinds of religion that develop subsequently. Totemism, Durkheim believed, contains within it all the major features which are found in even a highly elaborated creed such as Christianity. By studying totemism in some detail, we can thus reach conclusions of general application. Durkheim placed some considerable emphasis on this point. Just as valid and scientific as the comparative method in sociology is the careful analysis of a single, critically important phenomenon understood in all its aspects.

The basic mode of organization of the Australian societies in which totemism appears is a system of clan groups. The clan is marked by two characteristics. Those composing the clan regard themselves as each other's relatives, not in virtue of the fact that they have a definite blood relationship with one another, but because they share the same name. Second, this common name is the designation of a type of object, the totem, which has a very special significance to all members of the clan group. Every clan has its particular totem, shared with no other. The cosmic phenomena which seem to brook large in more developed religious systems – the sun, moon, stars, etc. – rarely appear as totems, although they do so occasionally. Totems are most often more humble objects in the immediate environment: animals or plants. The totem is usually not a particular object, but a class of objects, such as an animal species. A totem is much more than a mere name. It is believed to contain within itself the distinctive characteristics of the clan, and is the subject of numerous kinds of rites; and it is in connection with it that the universe is separated into the sacred and the profane. The totem, according to Durkheim, 'is the very prototype of sacred things'. (P. 140.) The sacred character of the totem object also extends to its image. Similar sorts of ritual observations to those involved with the totemic object surround representations of the totem inscribed on material artifacts or on the person; these are in fact frequently more strongly insisted upon than those which concern the totemic object as such. Besides the totem itself and the graphic representation of the totem, there is a third class of objects that possess sacred qualities. These are the members of the clan themselves. In the more developed religions, it is usually the case that most members of the religious community are profane beings, with only a specialized group of religious leaders or priests who participate more directly in the sphere of the sacred. This is not so in totemism.

The three types of objects recognized to possess sacred qualities, the totem, the sign of the totem, and the members of the clan, in totemism are each connected within a cosmological system. This is a crucial part of Durkheim's argument, and he used it to develop a thesis of genuine originality. The cosmologies involved in totemism, he pointed out, have largely been ignored by previous authors writing on the topic, because the latter have failed to understand the significance of the fact that the clan members possess sacred attributes. They do so on the basis of sharing an identity with the totem: the name which the individual shares with the totem denotes an identity in nature between the two. Most observers, coming from a European cultural background, have treated the clan as a group of men like any other. But the Australian does not draw the same distinction between man and nature as we do; the consistent elements of nature are parts of the tribe, as the members of the tribe are parts of nature. The totem provides the organizing principle for an ordered classification of the whole of the cosmos. A given object will be assigned to a particular clan as falling within its realm: it will have the same totem as the human members of the clan. A second object, or type of object, will belong to another clan. Thus the sun is classified under one totem, the moon under another, and so on, providing a complex and exhaustive classification of nature. Durkheim based this section of his analysis in *The Elementary Forms* on a study of primitive classification which he wrote together with Mauss, and published in the *Année Sociologique* in 1903. In the monograph they claimed to show that similar principles of classification to those involved in Australian totemism are found among the Zuñi and the Sioux of North America; and they also examined religion in traditional China and in Greece. Although there is no material available to document historically the evolution of the Chinese or Greek systems of classification from totemic forms, the basic principles, they argued, are the same. Mythologies are expressions of classification systems; thus the Greek gods had specific phenomena assigned to them, with the relations between the divinities identifying relations of co-ordination and hierarchy in nature as a whole. 'Primitive classifications', Durkheim and Mauss concluded, 'are therefore not singular or exceptional, having no analogy with those employed by more civilized peoples; on the contrary, they seem to be connected, with no break in continuity, to the first scientific classifications.'[5] Primitive classifications constitute a 'first philosophy of nature'. In the totemic systems of classification, the influence of religion is all-pervasive. In more developed forms of religion, when gods appear, each is at the head of a category of natural phenomena, which derives its energy from the god. At a later stage still, the gods themselves become dissolved, with the progress of the secularization of thought; the classifications originating in religion still, however, leave their imprint upon the scientific classifications that are later elaborated.

Since, in totemic beliefs, the scope of religious influences is so all-embracing, the sacred qualities which the totem possesses cannot derive from properties of the totemic object itself: the human members of the clan, and the image of the totem, are the subjects of the same sentiments as the totemic object. Their religious attributes must come from a source which is common to them all: an 'anonymous and impersonal force' which is found in each of these three beings, but which is not to be confused with any of them. In Australian totemism, this divine force is not abstractly separated, in the system of beliefs, from the objects in which it is made incarnate. Among somewhat more advanced societies it normally has a generic name: in Melanesia, it is called *mana*. 'The totemic principle', Durkheim concluded, 'can therefore be nothing else than the clan itself, personified and represented to the imagination under the visible form of the animal or vegetable which serves as the totem.' Society 'has all that is necessary to arouse the sensation of the divine', through the strength of the influence which it exerts over its individual members:

a god is, first of all, a being whom men think of as superior to themselves, and upon whom they feel that they depend. Whether it be a conscious personality, such as Zeus or Jahveh, or merely abstract forces such as those in play in totemism, the worshipper, in the one case as in the other, believes himself held to certain manners of acting which are imposed upon him by the nature of the sacred principle with which he feels he is in communion. (Pp. 236-7.)

Such an account does not explain why the religious force should become focused on a particular totem. This divides into two questions: why is there a totem at all, and why should a particular object become chosen as the totem? Each, according to Durkheim, is quite readily answered. The answer to the first is that the totem is the emblem of the clan; the sentiments produced by the dominance of society over the individual become attached to the totem as the most distinctive symbol of the group. This explains also why the image of the totem is treated as more sacred than the totemic object. The selection of a particular object as the totem simply reflects the things in the environment with which the group is most frequently in contact. In the Australian societies, animals are more often totems than plants or natural phenomena. This is because these are hunting and fishing societies; thus the animal is 'more closely associated with their life than the plant is'. (P. 266.) But it is an important aspect of Durkheim's theory that the objects which become invested with divine attributes are in some degree arbitrary, since those objects themselves are not the source of their sacred character. Any variety of otherwise entirely utilitarian objects can acquire a sacred character merely by their association with a deity. Thus the robe of Christ is sacred just because he wore it. Moreover, its sacred qualities do not depend upon the original identity of the object as such: the robe may become dismembered into fragments, each of which is just as holy as every other. This 'contagious' property of the sacred helps explain the systems of classification which develop around the totem : the sacred qualities of the totem become diffused outwards to the objects or phenomena with which it stands in a certain relation : e.g., the food it eats, vegetation in which it lives, etc.

Finally, we must explain the development of conceptions of god out of the diffuse idea of the religious which exists in totemism. There are in fact certain Australian tribes among whom a rudimentary conception of a god has developed. The main characteristics of this deity are in all cases the same. The god is an immortal being, who is secondary to no other; he is regarded as the creator of both man and nature. The idea of such a god is a logical development of totemism, 'implied in the very principles upon which totemism rests'. (P. 327.) Totemism tends to produce an attitude of veneration toward ancestors, as the source of the religiosity with which the members of the tribe are endowed. With the passing of the generations, these become treated as deities, with a supreme god who is the ancestor of all the others and the creator of the tribe itself.

It will be recalled that Durkheim insisted upon two elements in his definition of religion : the existence of sacred symbols and objects on the one hand, and on the other their connection with definite ceremonial practices organized through a church. So far the theory has identified the source of the first of these, but not that of the second. The sacred, as the exemplification of the power of society, involves the twin elements of morality : devotion and obligation. But how do these become engrained into the conduct of the individual members of the group? This is explained through the occurrences of regular collective ceremonial. The life of the Australian societies passes through cycles alternating religious ceremonial with utilitarian activity. For most of the year, each kinship group lives separately, devoting itself to economic ends. However, at definite times the members of the different clans gather together to participate in religious ceremonials. These phases of social activity sharply contrast with each other. Day-to-day life, involving hunting, fishing or gathering, is made up of ordinary, routine activities; the public ceremonials, by contrast, are highly intense and emotional in character. It is in the ferment of the ceremonial gathering that the collectivity impresses itself most overwhelmingly upon the individual: he is brought into a world which differs dramatically from his activity in the profane, utilitarian world of economic production. In such ceremonies, the sacred is created and recreated; in the states of exultation which are achieved, 'a man does not recognize himself any longer' and feels 'dominated and carried away by some sort of an external power which makes him think and act differently than in normal times'. (P. 249.) He participates as a sacred being, a transformation aided by the decorations with which he adorns himself, or the mask he wears. Religious ceremonial is both the source of innovation, under the stimulus of collective enthusiasm, and at the same time has the function of renewing faith in existing beliefs and symbols. It is because of the need to achieve such renewal that, in all religions, ceremonials take place in a recurrent or periodic manner. In the everyday activities of social life, where people are preoccupied with utilitarian tasks, pursuing their egoistic interests, the hold of the collectivity over individuals becomes weakened; religious ceremonial revives and sustains collective ideals.

In the simple societies, where such ideals are the main basis of social cohesion, collective ceremonial is thus fundamental to the sustaining of the continuity of the group.

Various kinds of rites are associated with ceremonial activity in totemism – aspects of which are found in all religions. Durkheim distinguished 'positive' rites from 'negative' ones. The latter are directed towards maintaining the sanctity of the sphere of the sacred, its distinctiveness in relation to the world of profane activity. Negative rites or taboos are interdictions that limit contact between the sacred and the profane, and prepare the individual for entry into the religious domain. The transition from one realm to the other is marked by the donning of special clothes or ornaments and by forms of abstinence or ordeal that have to be endured. All negative rites have one positive aspect, however: they sanctify the individual so that he is able to enter the sacred sphere. Thus there is not always a precise division between them and positive rites. The latter constitute the core of the ceremonial as such, and are the medium of achieving communion with the divine. In Australian totemism, the positive rites are typically organized in two phases in the ceremonial. In the first, rites are enacted whose goal is to ensure the prosperity of the animal or plant that serves as the totem. Following this, formal ritual activity is temporarily suspended, although states of religious enthusiasm remain at a high level. In the concluding phase of the ceremony, part of the totem is ritually eaten, and songs sung in praise of the exploits of past members of the clan, both human and non-human. This practice is the early origin of the institution of sacrifice, prominent in more developed religions. Sacrifice is an act of communion with the divine, allowing the communicant to share in the sacred properties of the object through consuming its flesh; it is simultaneously an offering made to the deity.

Ritual, which often consists of apparently trivial activities, derives its hold over those who enact it from the moral power which comes from the collective affirmation of beliefs and symbols that it helps to create. We can observe this phenomenon, Durkheim pointed out, even in religious ceremonial which occurs in the midst of highly secularized societies. Some of those who attend a Christian church regularly might be quite sceptical about the effect which certain rites are supposed to produce; but they nevertheless continue to observe them, sensing that they are integral to the process of collective moral affirmation.

> This is why the easy criticisms to which an unduly simple rationalism has sometimes submitted ritual prescriptions generally leave the believer indifferent: it is because the true justification of religious practices does not lie in the apparent ends they pursue, but rather in the invisible action which they exercise over the mind ... (P. 403.)

For the same reason, we find that rites are functionally equivalent to one another. That is to say, what the rite is, in terms of actual conduct, is relatively unimportant. It is what the rite does which matters: and all rites have one pre-eminent function, that of enhancing the solidarity of the group. Much the same formal rites thus can be used for marriages as for christenings.

Besides contrasting positive and negative rites, Durkheim also distinguished a third form: 'piacular' rites, which are especially associated with mourning. The collective effects of the ceremonial are the same as in the other forms, but the content of the sentiments aroused and sharpened by the presence of the group are different. Sadness or grief is the dominant emotion; among the Australian societies, rites of mourning produce a veritable 'panic of sorrow'. Piacular rites are not really another type alongside positive and negative rites, because they themselves have positive and negative aspects. Negative piacular rites consist in various kinds of absentions and prohibitions, such that the mourner is forbidden for a period to speak the name of the dead, or has to remain near the place where the death occurred, or must refrain from normal economic activity, etc. Positive rites include wailing, self-mutilation, and the wearing of special clothing. The burial ceremonial initiates ritual observances of each of these sorts; the bereaved have to maintain certain of them for a long period, sometimes lasting years, afterwards. According to Durkheim, mourning is not the spontaneous expression of grief, or at least it is only so for those personally affected by the death; mourning is a duty imposed by the group. The social function of mourning is to draw the group together when its solidarity is threatened by the loss of one of its members. The group reaffirms its own permanence in the face of the transitory nature of the life of the individual; and those most affected by the death are drawn into the centre of the community when they might otherwise feel most impelled to renounce it. The long-term rituals of mourning which the directly bereaved have to observe similarly force their private emotions into a publicly expressed form, thereby connecting their personal experience to group traditions: 'eventually one stops mourning, and one does so because of the mourning itself.' (P. 448.)

An essential part of the theory of religion advanced by Durkheim in *The Elementary Forms* is the thesis that, as he put it, 'there are no religions which are false'. The justifications which believers give as to why they believe what they do may be erroneous, but all religions express the conditions of social reality which generate them.

> Religious beliefs and practices undoubtedly seem disconcerting at times, and one is tempted to attribute them to some sort of a deep-seated error. But one must know how to go underneath the symbol to the reality which it represents and which gives it its meaning. (P. 14.)

This is what Durkheim tried to accomplish in his theory of knowledge, which is an attempt to find the origins of the basic categories of knowledge in social experience. The very notion of 'category' or 'class' itself, as the theory of primitive classification was intended to show, derives from society: 'the unity of these first logical systems merely reproduces the unity of the society.' (P. 170.) This does not imply that the perception of nature is completely determined by the organization of society. The systems of categorization elaborated around the totem depend upon certain biologically given sensory capacities: thus in the totemic classifications the night is placed together with the black cockatoo, the sun with the white cockatoo, or the totemic animal is associated with the things he eats. But the discrimination of such similarities and affinities is different, Durkheim avowed, from grasping the notion of a category of objects. The sensory input which is our experience of the world is composed of indistinct and mobile images; the idea of 'category' involves the formation of clear-cut logical oppositions or dichotomies. The concept of category is not an inherent property of the human mind; neither are the particular categories of space, time or causality, as Kant believed. These notions, in Durkheim's words, 'exist in an implicit way in individual consciousness': the individual lives in time and space, and reacts to the continuity of phenomena. But this is distinct from grasping the concepts of space, time and cause. Concepts are not, like experiences, particular to individuals; they are shared by the members of the group, and must therefore have initially been derived from features of the life of the collectivity. The concept of efficient cause derives from the action of collective or divine force. The idea of time and its subdivisions originates in the periodic occurrence of ceremonial; that of space in the territory occupied by the tribe. The latter can be illustrated by the fact that, in the Australian societies space is conceived as a gigantic circle, reflecting the shape of the encampment; and the reorganized abstract divisions of space exactly mirror the division of the community circle into clan territories. Society is thus the source of the impersonal character of thought, as being on a level removed from individual experiences and whims. The impersonal nature of thought is in turn closely connected with truth, which is accepted as holding independent of individual volition. The idea of truth has thence, of course, become fundamental to science, and to the evolution of a secularized world-view.

In *The Elementary Forms*, Durkheim made no attempt to trace out directly the changes which religion undergoes with the process of social development. It is important to relate the remarks he did make in the conclusion of the work to the context of his general views on the nature of the modern social order, as I have outlined the latter previously.

> There is something eternal in religion [he wrote toward the end of the study] which is destined to survive all the particular symbols in which religious thought has successfully enveloped itself. There can be no society which does not feel the need of upholding and reaffirming at regular intervals the collective sentiments and the collective ideas which give it its unity and individuality. (Pp. 474-5.)

Such statements, taken in isolation, might be thought to imply that Durkheim came to reject the notion that the moral order of contemporary society must be distinctively different from that of the past. But this would undoubtedly be a misreading. If religion, as a social phenomenon, has something eternal in it, this does not consist in the gods of the traditional religious systems. The persisting elements of religion concern the necessarily moral character of all social relations, and the pre-eminence of society as the fount of all that makes man human. The thesis that 'the old gods are growing old or already dead' is vigorously reiterated. Comte was wrong to suppose that 'the old historic souvenirs can be artificially revived'. (P. 475.) Religion has two essential ideational components: on the one side the provision of moral ideals and moral regulation, and on the other the creation of a cognitive framework whereby the world can be understood conceptually. The ideals of moral individualism become the core of the first. The second becomes more and more the province of science. Scientific thought introduces features that are largely absent from religious cosmologies, including systematic empirical method and a critical spirit; but the concepts elaborated in science have their origin in religious representations, and evolve from them in direct line of continuity. Insofar as religion concerns conduct, and its moral basis, science cannot replace it. But the critical and rationalist spirit that becomes central to science also inevitably pervades the general area of morality. From the present day onwards, 'faith no longer exercises the same hegemony as formerly over the system of ideas that we can continue to call religion. A rival power rises up before it which, being born of it, ever after submits it to its criticism and control.' (P. 479.)

6 Critical Commentary

Having tried, so far, to provide a descriptive account of Durkheim's writings, I shall now attempt a brief, but general critique of them. I shall base this discussion on the four major books which were published in Durkheim's lifetime: *The Division of Labour*, *The Rules*, *Suicide* and *The Elementary Forms*. Although these form part of a much larger corpus of work, with which they are closely connected, they are the most important part, and can serve as a focus for ideas introduced in his other writings.

The Elementary Forms was written at the initial stages of the development of modern anthropological field-work, and it is not surprising that the empirical basis of the work today appears suspect.[1] Durkheim used as a case-study Australian totemism which, he believed, being the simplest type of religious system known, would clarify the main elements of religion as a whole. Subsequent research indicates, however, that the totemism of the tribes to which Durkheim referred most extensively, those inhabiting Central Australia, is not even typical of Australian totemism as a whole, let alone totemic systems in other parts of the world. Some of the features of central Australian totemism to which Durkheim gave particular prominence, such as the regularized ceremonial activities, are either absent, or exist in quite different form elsewhere. Moreover, many anthropologists today no longer accept that totemism is a form of religion at all, but see it as a form of ritual and kinship organization, which can coexist with a series of religious institutions. These observations are damaging to Durkheim's arguments, although they do not necessarily compromise them completely. However there is another empirical consideration which has direct and serious implications for the basic ideas in his theory of religion. Durkheim's definition of religion depends upon the polarity of the sacred and profane, as discrete and opposed spheres. But although such a polarity can be clearly discerned in certain religious systems, particularly those of Judaeo-Christian origins, it is by no means universal. On the contrary, it seems that more often than not what Durkheim distinguished as the sacred and the profane intermingle in everyday conduct.

One hardly needs to stress the significance of this latter point. In coming to the view of the universal disjunction of the sacred and the profane, Durkheim believed he had validated his theory of moral authority. The notion of dual character of morality, as constraining and satisfying, is supposed to be exemplified by the scared/profane dichotomy, as is the idea of *homo duplex*. Moreover, as the focal point of Durkheim's definition of religion, the distinction of the sacred and the profane is applied to substantiate the view that religion has nothing to do intrinsically with the existence of gods or spirits. This in turn is vital to the thesis that religion must survive, in some guise or another, in all societies: i.e., that moral individualism is a form of religion.

Critics have sometimes said that Durkheim's theory of religion demonstrates no sensitivity to change, being concerned above all with the functions of religion in sustaining social cohesion. Thus expressed, such a statement is scarcely accurate. His work on religion dovetails into a continuing preoccupation with the contrasts – and the continuities – between the traditional types of society and the contemporary industrial order. Moreover, the collective ferment of religious ceremonial is not only the means of reaffirming already accepted beliefs and symbols, it is the source of the creation of new ones. This having been said, there is much to quarrel with in the manner in which Durkheim connected religion and social change. The assumptions of his evolutionary scheme today seem naïve. Totemism is selected as the simplest known form of religion, existing in the simplest known form of society; and it is presumed that the beliefs and practices found there represent religion stripped to its essentials. But these premises are each questionable. It does not follow that the simplest religion will be found in the simplest society, nor is this idea borne out by subsequent evidence. It is only if one presumes that the essential core of an institution remains unchanged through all subsequent processes of social change, that it might follow that complex social systems can best be illuminated by the study of the most primitive types. There is a more fundamental point to be made than any of these, however: one which connects with the major preoccupations of Durkheim's sociology. Basing his theory of religion on a structurally very simple society, where the clan is the major subdivision, and where there are no distinct religious leaders or functionaries, reinforced Durkheim's defined tendency to speak of 'society' as a homogeneous entity. In the whole of Durkheim's writings, he nowhere confronts the possibility that religious beliefs are ideologies, which help legitimate the domination of some groups over others. The notion which pervades Max Weber's writings on the sociology of religion, that religious beliefs legitimize discrete group interests, is hence almost completely absent from Durkheim's theory of religion.

An illuminating contrast can be made if we compare Durkheim's view of religion with the discussions of religion which appear in the writings of Feuerbach and Marx. Feuerbach's theory of religion shares some affinities with that advanced by Durkheim. For the former, religion is the worship of values created by human society. But religion is at the same time the expression of human self-alienation, a barrier to the real accomplishment of the ideals that are removed to a mystical sphere. In Marx, of course, religion appears as a medium of the domination of asymmetrical class interests. In both cases, however, it is held that religious values embody mystified ideals which can only be actualized by social critique. Whatever the validity of such a conception, it is one which demands serious debate. Durkheim did not consider it at all. He had really precluded such consideration from the beginning, as a result of his insistence that 'religion cannot be false', because it expresses aspects of social reality, and corresponds to definite functional needs. But a system of religious beliefs may relate to the 'needs' of a society in which there are gaping inequalities of power and wealth, which it thereby serves to sanction.

Let me turn briefly to the theory of knowledge which Durkheim elaborated in the context of his sociology of religion. Few aspects of his writings have played a greater part in the subsequent formation of modern social thought. The thesis that modalities of knowledge originate in the symbolic classification of objects is at least one major source of some of the leading currents in contemporary structuralism. However Durkheim's attempt to 'sociologize' Kant as such is plainly deficient. His argument is that the categories of thought are derived from the organization of the collectivity, such that the idea of time is acquired from 'social time', that of space from 'social space', etc. But a Kantian could simply reply that the recognition of social time or social space already presupposes the discriminations which it purports to explain; one could not grasp concepts of time and space without possessing the faculty of organizing one's experience in these terms. Whatever view we take of Kant's philosophy as such, Durkheim's theory does not provide a counter to it.

Just as it is sometimes remarked that Durkheim's theory of religion is unconcerned with the influence of religion on social change, so it is often alleged that his interpretation of religion – and indeed his sociology more generally – ignores the phenomenon of social conflict. In any straightforward sense, this is again manifestly not the case. Durkheim was in fact deeply concerned with the turmoil affecting the European societies in his time. But he always tended to conceptualize conflict in terms of oppositions between the individual and the collectivity, rather than between interest groups in a system of domination and subordination. When Durkheim spoke of 'interests' he did so usually in the context of the push-and-pull of egoism versus altruism: the interests of the individual in conflict with those of the social community as a whole. The notion that society could be conceptualized as a system of groups chronically in tension is foreign to his viewpoint, which treats societies as unified wholes (regardless of whether the basis of such unity is traced to mechanical or to organic solidarity). Conflict or division of interest between groups is treated only as a phenomenon of transitional phases in social development, in which the alignment of functions is temporarily out of equilibrium. In Durkheim's writings, religious prescriptions, and moral norms more generally, are discussed as if they were capable of only one mode of interpretation by the members of society. But a single set of symbols and codes, such as those involved in Christian dogma can, and ordinarily do, become the subject of variant and antagonistic interpretations, likely to be tied in to the struggles of divergent interest-groups.

Similar comments can be made in respect of Durkheim's theory of moral obligation or discipline. In his later writings on the subject, as I have mentioned in a previous chapter, Durkheim distinguished two senses of 'sanction': those associated with moral phenomena, which constitute the type case of social sanctions generally, and those associated with natural events. The obligatory character of moral conduct derives fundamentally from the acceptance of the twin elements of respect and self-restraint that moral codes engender. Natural constraints or 'utilitarian sanctions', on the other hand, have consequences that flow 'mechanically' from an act. The distinction is an interesting and important one, but it glosses over one highly significant difference between the two types, which it could readily have been used to bring out. Utilitarian sanctions have their effects regardless of how those involved in contravening them define the character of their act. This is not so with the operation of moral sanctions, where the interpretation of the meaning of codes of morality, and of action oriented to them, may be a matter of contention between individuals or groups. Thus a person may be intensely committed to a particular moral ideal, but believe that it is currently defined or interpreted in a degraded or mistaken way. Such a situation often characterizes the rise of sectarian or oppositional religious or political movements. Conversely, in other circumstances, moral sanctions can operate in much more of a 'utilitarian' fashion, for much of the population much of the time, than Durkheim was prepared to acknowledge. That is to say, reigning moral codes may be treated as posing risks of sanction that have to be run if they are not observed, but as not legitimately 'moral', as having no morally binding force upon conduct. For Durkheim, this is inevitably regarded as 'demoralization' or anomie; but it may perhaps be more appropriately regarded as reflecting the domination of some groups, and the interests which they wish to legitimate, over others.

Durkheim's use of the notion of anomie tends to assimilate two discrete senses in which human aims or aspirations may be 'unrealizable'. One is the sense in which needs have no intrinsic limits or 'ceiling'. The other is that in which aspirations cannot be realized in a definite social setting, or form of society, because that society creates potentialities which are incapable of actualization within the existing social framework. The difference is a consequential one. Insofar as an author accentuates the latter type of conception, rather than the first, his analysis is led towards an emphasis upon the strains or contradictions brought about by social development, and their relev-

ance to demands for further social transformation.
Insofar as the first kind of view is stressed, by contrast, one is led to emphasize an intrinsic opposition
between man and society, such that moral norms must
restrain the inherent insatiability of human desires.
The more recent literature in which the concept of
anomie has been taken over from Durkheim and
elaborated by other authors indicates how the notion
can be developed in different directions. Some have used
'anomie' as equivalent to 'normlessness', thus inclining
towards the first type of interpretation of the concept;
such a view tends to treat social conflict as the result
of incomplete moral consensus, and to trace the sources
of 'deviance' to 'imperfect socialization' or incomplete
moral development. Others have tended towards the
second type of interpretation, using 'anomie' to mean
'normative strain' rather than 'normlessness': i.e., a
situation where the moral values or norms which are
accepted by the members of a group are not matched
by the possibilities of realizing the goals thus affirmed.[2]

Each of these versions of the idea of anomie is
present in *The Division of Labour*, and although in his
later writings Durkheim tried to resolve the difficulties
which this created for his analysis of the emergence
of the modern industrial order, he did not manage
successfully to do so. The reasons undoubtedly derive
in some part from the intrinsic limitations of his theory
of the division of labour itself. The division of labour
is treated as inherently a source of solidarity; if the
division of labour produces conflict, it is either because
society is in a transitional state of development, or it
denotes the existence of a pathological condition of
the social order. This thesis is in turn related to the
biological analogy frequently employed in *The Division*

of Labour. The simpler societies are compared to simple organisms, the more complex ones to organic unities, in which the parts of the body are functionally linked together as an integrated system. The expansion of the division of labour, in its 'normal form', is supposed to be akin to the functional differentiation of the organism. Thus there is no room for the idea that the division of labour, in the advanced societies, might be more adequately regarded as a system of groups, or classes, in tension deriving from endemic division of interest. The division of labour, Durkheim asserted, 'spontaneously' produces solidarity – so long as 'external' inequalities are removed, and the relations between occupational groups are morally regulated. This is why he did not give much attention to the factors which might obstruct the dissolution of external inequalities: with a gentle push from the state, such inequalities will disappear of their own accord as organic solidarity becomes securely established.

Durkheim's account of the modern state, and of the role the occupational associations are to play in contemporary society, reflect the deficiencies of his theory of the division of labour. For Durkheim, the state is above all a moral agency, which concentrates within itself the values of the broader social community, giving them a clarity of focus that cannot be achieved by the community as a whole. Again the biological parallel is used: the state is the 'brain', the co-ordinating mechanism, of the social organism. In *Professional Ethics and Civic Morals*, which contains a full-scale discussion of the state, the proposition that the latter institution acts to preserve existing relations of domination and subordination is not even considered; Durkheim took it for granted that the state, in the 'normal' form of organic solidarity at least, represents the interests of the mass of the population. The fact that the corporations have not developed in Western societies in the manner in which Durkheim anticipated, however, indicates the persisting character of conflict within the division of labour. The unions have remained largely 'conflict organizations', rather than becoming the moral associations which Durkheim envisaged; the strike continues to be basic to the relations of power between the unions and employers. As Georges Friedmann has remarked, if Durkheim lived today he 'would have been obliged to consider "abnormal" most of the forms taken by labour in modern society both in industry and in administration . . .'[8]

Durkheim did acknowledge that the power of the state can become autocratic; hence his stress upon the occupational associations intervening between the state and the individual. But his conception of democracy is a direct continuation of the themes of his analysis of the modern state and reflects its deficiencies. Democracy concerns the closeness of contact that is sustained between the population and their rulers. Two sets of facts that seem fundamental to a democratic society are wholly absent from this idea of democracy. One is the notion that a democratic order provides for the expression of sectional group interests; the other is that, in a democracy, those over whom political power is wielded are able in some way directly to influence its exercise. The first is really precluded by the emphases noted previously : persistent opposition of interest is not recognized as a characteristic of the contemporary social order; the state expresses the interests of the collectivity as a whole. Durkheim explicitly wrote off the second as having any relevance to modern, complex societies. The mass of the population today can have no chance of either participating in, or even of immediately influencing, the taking of the decisions to which it is subject. But against this it can reasonably be argued that we should not dismiss the idea of what has come to be called 'participatory democracy' so readily – although its realization might require more far-reaching changes in the institutions of society than Durkheim foresaw as either desirable or necessary.[4]

Durkheim was surely correct to separate off the socialist doctrines which sprung up from the late eighteenth century onwards from the carefully constructed utopias of Plato, More and other early thinkers. But the point is not a particularly original one, and was made forcibly by Marx in distinguishing his political theory from various types of 'utopian socialism'. The question really at issue is whether or not it is plausible to regard socialist ideas as being principally concerned with the need for regulating the modern economy, the preoccupation with transcending systems of class domination being of secondary importance. The short answer is that it is not plausible to do so. The analysis which Durkheim offered of socialist philosophies is only persuasive if one accepts the theory of the division of labour which is its foundation. Durkheim's attempt to recharacterize socialism in his own terms is typical of his style of argument. The division of labour, once morally regulated, produces social solidarity. Socialism is an expression of the awareness of the need for such regulation; but socialist doctrines also contain proposals for fundamental social change, including the transcendence of the division of labour, as the means of superseding class domination. Since the latter elements do not accord with Durkheim's diagnosis of the social changes called for in contemporary society, they are treated not merely as detachable from the issue of regulation, but are made extraneous to the very definition of 'socialism' as such. The leading socialist doctrines were not, as Durkheim asserted, primarily concerned with economic regulation in pursuit of economic ends. In this respect Durkheim forced socialist theories into a conceptual niche which he had prepared for them. In anticipating the overthrow of capitalism, Marx, for example, presaged the overcoming both of class domination and of the subordination of human life to economic ends.

Throughout his writings, Durkheim was concerned with distinguishing the 'normal' from the 'pathological' in the contemporary social world. Such a concern ties together his analysis of the emergence of organic solidarity with his more abstract discussions of ethical philosophy. It is no use, he believed, attempting to establish ethical precepts in separation from the context of the operation of moral rules within definite types of society. But he developed this idea in two partly distinct ways. Sometimes he argued only that a comparative, scientific study of different forms of morality must constitute the material basis for a philosophy of ethics. This would imply that ethical philosophy cannot stand apart from the empirical study of moral conduct, but would nevertheless recognize the dualism of fact and value : such a philosophy cannot be directly derived from comparative sociology. More often, however, he was inclined to argue that sociological analysis can bridge the separation of fact and value by showing that what is normal for a definite type of society has a positive moral value for it. Neither view, however, is particularly convincing, or well formulated philosophically. If we accept the dualism of fact and value, no amount of comparative empirical material, however systematic it may be, will resolve problems as to how we should act. The idea that sociology can accomplish similar tasks to applied medicine, in diagnosing maladies of the social organism, on the other hand, hardly supplies, as Durkheim believed, a means of transcending the philosophical argument for the dichotomy of fact and value. According to Durkheim, sociology can furnish a scientific diagnosis of social pathology, as medicine can of physical disease. But the advocate of the traditional philosophical standpoint would simply reply that medicine is not able in fact to identify what 'illness' is through the methods of empirical science; the norms of health and pathology involve values which are not justified by medical science, but on the contrary provide the ends to which medicine is the means.

One of Durkheim's main arguments for distinguishing sociology from other types of social theory or social philosophy (e.g., socialism) was that the progress of science is slow and fragmentary. The great socialist thinkers wanted to establish overall schemes of social change, the claims involved in which go far beyond what has been reliably documented about social life. Sociology, Durkheim suggested, must be more modest and cautious in its recommendations for practical reform, as befits a science. This was also the origin of some of his criticisms of the work of those he recognized as his predecessors in the development of sociology, such as Comte and Spencer; they had laid claim to founding a science of society, but their writings ranged much more broadly than would have been the case if they had really been concerned with the detailed empirical validation of their theories. However Durkheim's writings are surely open to the same objection which he levelled against others. He was just as prone as they were to claim as scientifically proven theories which conformed to his own moral and political aims. The thesis that the division of labour is inherently harmonious, or that new forms of occupational association are destined to emerge in contemporary society, are apt cases in point.

More than any other single work, *Suicide* was planned by Durkheim to be a concrete demonstration of the principles of his conception of sociological method. In conclusion, therefore, it seems appropriate to consider some of the failings of Durkheim's theory of suicide, looked at from the perspective of today. For the sake of brevity I shall concentrate upon the following points, which are in ascending order of importance in terms of their implications for the evaluation of his conception of sociological method: his dismissal of non-social influences on suicide; his reliance upon official suicide statistics in order to document his hypotheses; and the form of his explanatory account of the causation of suicide.

In the opening chapter of *Suicide*, Durkheim tried to show that 'non-social' factors, such as climate, race, etc., have no influence upon the distribution of suicide. He did so by considering them separately from one another, as part of an 'argument by elimination'. Suicide rates do not show a close correlation with any one such type of factor; hence we have to conclude that only social influences can explain the incidence of suicide. As many critics have pointed out, the con-

clusion does not follow.⁵ The most Durkheim can claim
to have shown is that no one such non-social phenomenon can explain observed differences in suicide
rates; his analysis does not demonstrate that they have
no influence upon suicide rates at all, or that acting
in combination they might not have a strong influence
upon suicide. The point has more than a purely pro-
cedural significance, since it bears upon Durkheim's
proneness to draw very precise lines between what is
'social' and what is not, and to suppose that this also
presupposes clear-cut causal boundaries between classes
of phenomena. Either a phenomenon has an exclusively
social cause, or it is caused by a different type of factor
altogether.

Durkheim's use of suicide statistics in his study, as
I have pointed out earlier, owed a good deal to the
ideas of the 'moral statisticians'. Like them, Durkheim
looked to official statistics as an exact measure of the
distribution of suicide, and virtually the whole of his
work is based upon them. Even prior to Durkheim's
study, there had been lengthy debates about the usefulness of official statistics for the investigation of
suicide. Durkheim did not mention this controversy
in his work and barely considered the problem of the
validity of such statistics at all. But there are reasons
why we should have strong reservations about the use
of official statistics in research into suicide. Three of
these are worth mentioning here. The most often discussed, but least subtle, is the issue of how accurate
the official suicide statistics are. Durkheim was certainly much too sanguine, as however many others
have been before and since, about the use of the suicide statistics. It might be the case, for example, that
if we show a relationship between social integration

and suicide, this operates via dissimulation in the
collation of suicide statistics: the more strongly integrated the community, the more suicide is seen as a
disgrace by those close to the person concerned, and
consequently the greater pressure to conceal suicide
as a likely cause of death. Such an interpretation is
not perhaps particularly plausible; more important is
the consideration that the designation 'suicide' demands
a process of inference, often on the basis of scanty,
and necessarily *ex post facto* evidence, as to why the
person acted as he did. A suicide is not just a death,
but a death which the individual in some sense intended
to bring about (although, as I shall shortly mention,
Durkheim tried to define 'suicide' without reference to
intentions). The identification of a death as a suicide
thus involves a reconstruction of the person's probable
state of mind prior to the act of self-destruction, ad-
judged in terms of the motives that 'typically' lead
to such an act. Now at least some of the differences
found in suicide rates between different countries, or
areas within the same country, might be the result of
divergences in the assessment of 'evidence' by the
relevant officials. If the modes of making such assessment differ in standard, regularized ways, we will
obviously find stable divergences between suicide rates:
differences which reflect customary ways of collecting
and interpreting material on the circumstances surrounding death, rather than variations in the incidence
of suicide as such.

This leads us to a second type of consideration about
the application of official statistics to the study of
suicide. A suicide rate is more than an index of the
incidence of self-destructive acts. It is a social fact in
itself, the outcome of a complex set of events involving

numerous social actors: relatives, friends, doctors, police, coroners, etc. These phenomena cannot be studied by means of suicide statistics, because they are involved in the very creation of such statistics.[6] But if they are not studied directly, the most important area of social interaction relevant to the occurrence of suicide escapes analysis – as indeed it does in Durkheims' work, which concentrates on correlating suicide rates with generalized characteristics of group formation. The significance of this can be better illuminated if we pass to a third observation: that Durkheim concerned himself only with the statistics of completed suicide, neglecting attempted suicide. Such a neglect could be justified if it were the case that completed suicide were an integral phenomenon, distinctively different from suicide attempts that do not culminate in death. Even given the literature available in Durkheim's time this was not a credible view, and subsequent research has shown clearly that the study of attempted suicide is quite fundamental to the understanding of completed suicidal acts. This is easy to see if one considers suicide, not as an isolated deed, but the culmination of a long-term process of interaction between the individual concerned and others around him. Many individuals contemplating suicide give verbal warnings of the possibility, when beset by worries or anxieties. How far a person proceeds any further towards an attempt on his life may depend upon the response he receives from others to the signs that he is in difficulties. A considerable proportion of those attempting suicide do so in ways in which there is a strong element of 'risk-taking', leaving the outcome of the act contingent upon the potential intervention of others.[7] Thus whether or not an act becomes a 'suicide' does not simply depend upon elements intrinsic to the act itself, but upon other features of the social context involved – and, beyond them, upon the complex of events which intervene between the act and its possible appearance as a suicide statistic.

In *The Rules*, Durkheim argued that the first task of any sociological investigation is to provide a clear definition of the phenomenon to be studied. He followed this maxim in all of his own empirical studies, including *Suicide*. Suicide is defined as referring to 'all cases of death resulting directly or indirectly from a positive or negative act of the victim himself, which he knows will produce this result'.[8] The definition is related in a direct way to the character of the explanatory scheme which he then proceeded to develop. By substituting 'know' for 'intend', Durkheim effectively defined as irrelevant the intentions or reasons for which the act is undertaken. But there is a basic difference between doing something knowing a particular consequence is likely to follow, or may be unavoidable, and doing something intending that such a consequence should follow.[9] Durkheim wanted to bracket together suicidal conduct, as ordinarily understood, with acts in which individuals engage even though they realize their behaviour may very well eventuate in their death (but do not wish it), such as that of a soldier who obeys an order to charge the enemy in the face of overwhelming odds. He opted for such a concept of suicide because of the emphasis he placed upon external constraint, upon social causes which act from 'outside' the individual actor, regardless of his intentions, and impel him towards self-destruction. One comment that could be made about Durkheim's definition of suicide is that it is largely irrelevant to the material, i.e., official suicide statistics, upon which most of *Suicide* is based, for the lay notion of suicide certainly involves reference to self-destruction as a purposive act, and this is the sort of notion no doubt used by investigators who have produced the statistics. More important is that his theory of suicide does not allow room for the idea of the rationalized character of human action: the intrinsic feature of human conduct that actors reflexively 'monitor' their behaviour in conjunction with its purposive content. In other words, it is a deterministic theory, which treats suicide as the outcome of social causes, as these operate on particular types of individuals.

Durkheim's injunction that we should treat social phenomena as 'things' was supposed to be a methodological principle rather than an ontological one: we should approach the study of social facts as we do objects and events in nature, as if we were ignorant of their characteristic properties. But the social world is not like the world of nature in this sense. In studying society, we are dealing with a pre-interpreted world, sustained as such by the active efforts of its members. The condition on which we may enter this world, and describe its characteristics, is that we grasp the meaningful character of social activity. Consider, for example, the notion of suicide. 'Suicide' has not been invented by the sociologist, as 'particle acceleration' has by the physicist, nor does the latter concept presuppose that the subjects whose activity is thus referred to themselves understand the notion which describes their behaviour. A person cannot be said to 'commit suicide' if he kills himself accidentally, through engaging in an activity of whose lethal consequences he was ignorant. The existence of suicide, as an intentional act of self-destruction – and phenomenon available for sociological investigation – involves cultural meanings that actors themselves understand and apply in their own action.

To meet this point, it would not be enough however just to reverse Durkheim's precept, and declare that social facts are not things.[10] In seeking to demonstrate the influence of social causation upon human conduct, and in combating subjectivism, Durkheim was undoubtedly justified. These emphases must be sustained, but they cannot be satisfactorily elucidated within Durkheim's own scheme of sociological method.

Notes

(Page numbers from Durkheim's works cited in these Notes are not necessarily drawn either from the first translated editions or from the latest reprints. For details of the original publication of these works, the reader is referred to the Bibliography on page 124.)

INTRODUCTION

1. Davy, in *Centenaire de la naissance de Durkheim, Annales de l'Université de Paris*, no. 1, 1960, p. 15.
2. Contribution to 'Enquête sur l'influence allemande: II – sociologie et économie politique', *Mercure de France*, vol. 44, 1902, p. 647.
3. 'Cours de science sociale: leçon d'ouverture', *Revue internationale de l'enseignement*, vol. 15, 1888.
4. Quoted in Steven Lukes: *Emile Durkheim, his Life and Work*, London, 1973, p. 299.
5. 'Lettres au directeur de la revue néo-scolastique', *Revue néo-scolastique*, vol. 14, 1907, p. 402.

1 EARLY WORK

1. *The Division of Labour in Society*, London, 1964, p. 32. All further quotations in this chapter are from this work. Throughout the book I have modified translations if they seemed to me inaccurate or poorly expressed.
2. See, for example, Talcott Parsons: *The Structure of Social Action*, Glencoe, 1949, p. 304; Robert A. Nisbet, *Emile Durkheim*, Englewood Cliffs, 1965, p. 37.
3. cf. my 'Classical social theory and the origins of modern sociology', *American Journal of Sociology*, vol. 81, 1976.

2 SOCIOLOGICAL METHOD

1. *The Division of Labour*, op. cit., p. 273.
2. *Montesquieu and Rousseau*, Ann Arbor, 1960, p. 68.
3. *The Rules of Sociological Method*. London, 1964, p. xlviii. Other quotations up to note 4 are from this work.
4. cf. my article, 'The suicide problem in French sociology', *British Journal of Sociology*, vol. 16, 1965.
5. *Suicide: a Study in Sociology*, London, 1952, p. 46. Subsequent quotations in this chapter are from this source.

3 THE STATE AND POLITICS

1. Marcel Mauss: 'Introduction' to the first edition of *Socialism*. New York, 1962, p. 32. Further quotations are from this work.
2. cf. Georges Sorel: 'Les théories de M. Durkheim', *Le Devenir Social*, vol. 1, 1895 (two parts).
3. Max Weber: *Economy and Society*, New York, 1968, vol. 1, p. 342.
4. *Professional Ethics and Civic Morals*, London, 1958, p. 45.
5. 'L'Allemagne au-dessus de tout', Paris, 1915.

4 MORAL AUTHORITY AND EDUCATION

1. Letter to Davy, quoted in the latter's 'Emile Durkheim', *Revue française de sociologie*, vol. 1, 1960, p. 10.
2. For a contrasting discussion, cf. Ernest Wallwork: *Durkheim, Morality and Milieu*, Cambridge (Mass.), 1972.
3. *Sociology and Philosophy*, New York, 1974, p. 45. Subsequent quotations prior to note 4 are from this source.
4. *Moral Education*, London, 1961, p. 34.
5. 'The dualism of human nature and its social conditions', in Kurt H. Wolff: *Essays on Sociology and Philosophy*, New York, 1964, p. 326.
6. *Sociology and Philosophy*, op. cit., p. 72.
7. Quotations from *Moral Education*, op. cit., pp. 52 and 115.
8. *Education and Sociology*, London, 1956, p. 71.
9. *Moral Education*, op. cit., p. 160.
10. *Ibid.*, p. 183.
11. *L'Evolution pédagogique en France*, Paris, 1969, pp. 36-7.
12. *Ibid.*, p. 381.

5 RELIGION AND THE THEORY OF KNOWLEDGE

1. 'La science positive de la morale en Allemagne', *Revue philosophique*, vol. 24, 1887, pp. 116 and 120.
2. See especially *The Division of Labour, op. cit.*, pp. 168-72.
3. Talcott Parsons: *The Structure of Social Action, op. cit.*
4. *The Elementary Forms of the Religious Life*, New York, 1965, p. 55. Further quotations when not annotated are from this work.
5. *Primitive Classification*, London, 1963, p. 81.

6 CRITICAL COMMENTARY

1. For a useful summary of the critical reception of Durkheim's theory of religion, cf. Lukes, *op. cit.*, pp. 477ff.
2. cf. Talcott Parsons: *The Social System*, London, 1951, *passim*; R. K. Merton: 'Social structure and anomie' in *Social Theory and Social Structure*, Glencoe, 1957.
3. Georges Friedmann: *The Anatomy of Work*, London, 1961, p. 75.
4. cf. P. Baccrach: *The Theory of Democratic Elitism.*
5. See, e.g., Lukes, *op. cit.*, pp. 31-2.
6. cf. Jack D. Douglas: *The Social Meanings of Suicide*, Princeton, 1967.
7. Erwin Stengel: *Suicide and Attempted Suicide*, London, 1964.
8. *Suicide, op. cit.*, p. 44.
9. cf. Alasdair MacIntyre: 'The idea of a social science', *Aristotelian Society Supplement*, vol. 41, 1967.
10. Jules Monnerot, one of Durkheim's critics, made this phrase the title of his book: *Les faits sociaux ne sont pas des choses*, Paris, 1946.

Bibliography of Durkheim's Major Works

ORIGINAL WORKS

(Virtually all of Durkheim's books, including those which appeared posthumously, were first published in Paris by Felix Alcan.)

1893 *De la division du travail social: étude sur l'organisation des sociétés supérieures.*

1895 *Les règles de la méthode sociologique.*

1897 *Le suicide: étude de sociologie.*

1903 (with Marcel Mauss) 'De quelques formes primitives de classification: contribution a l'étude des représentations collectives', *L'Année sociologique*, vol. 6.

1912 *Les formes élémentaires de la vie religieuse: le système totémique en Australie.*

Published posthumously

1922 *Education et sociologie.* Introduction by Paul Fauconnet.

1924 *Sociologie et philosophie.* Preface by Celestin Bouglé.

1925 *L'Education morale.*

1928 *Le socialisme: sa définition, ses débuts, la doctrine Saint-Simonienne.* Introduction by Marcel Mauss.

1938 *L'Evolution pédagogique en France.* Introduction by Maurice Halbwachs; two volumes.

1950 *Leçons de sociologie: physique des moeurs et du droit.* Foreword by H. Nail Kubali; introduction by Georges Davy.

1955 *Pragmatisme et sociologie.* Reconstructed from students' notes by Armand Cuvillier; not yet translated.

Bibliography of Durkheim's Major Works

ENGLISH TRANSLATIONS

1915   *The Elementary Forms of the Religious Life: a Study in Religious Sociology.* Trans. Joseph Ward Swain (London: Allen & Unwin; New York: Macmillan).

1933   *The Division of Labour in Society.* Trans. with an introduction by George Simpson (New York: Macmillan).

1938   *The Rules of Sociological Method.* Trans. Sarah A. Solovay and John H. Mueller; introduction by George E. G. Catlin (Chicago: University of Chicago Press).

1951   *Suicide: a Study in Sociology.* Trans. John A. Spaulding and George Simpson; introduction by George Simpson (Glencoe: Free Press; London: Routledge & Kegan Paul, 1952).

1953   *Sociology and Philosophy.* Trans. D. F. Pocock; introduction by J. G. Peristiany (London: Cohen & West; Glencoe: Free Press).

1956   *Education and Sociology.* Trans. with an introduction by Sherwood D. Fox; Foreword by Talcott Parsons (Glencoe: Free Press).

1957   *Professional Ethics and Civic Morals.* Translation of *Leçons de Sociologie* by Cornelia Brookfield (London: Routledge & Kegan Paul).

1958   *Socialism and Saint-Simon* (subsequently entitled *Socialism*). Trans. Charlotte Sattler; introduction by Alvin W. Gouldner (Yellow Springs: Antioch Press; London: Routledge & Kegan Paul, 1959).

1960   *Montesquieu and Rousseau.* Trans. Ralph Manheim (Ann Arbor: University of Michigan Press).

1961   *Moral Education: a Study in the Theory and Application of the Sociology of Education.* Trans. Everett K. Wilson and Herman Schnurer; introduction by Everett K. Wilson (Glencoe: Free Press).

1963   *Primitive Classification.* Trans. with an introduction by Rodney Needham (London: Cohen & West; Chicago: University of Chicago Press).

1977   *The Evolution of Educational Thought.* Trans. Peter Collins (London: Routledge & Kegan Paul).

THE LIFE AND DEATH OF ST KILDA

Tom Steel

On 29 August 1930, the remaining 36 inhabitants of this bleak but spectacular island group off the western coast of Scotland took ship for the mainland. Until the evacuation St Kilda was the most remote inhabited part of the United Kingdom, and indeed one of the most isolated points of the British Empire; its inhabitants had more in common with the people of Tristan da Cunha than they ever had with their fellow Scots in Glasgow or Edinburgh. The St Kildans had preserved a unique and unchanging way of life for centuries; untroubled by the fluctuations of events on the mainland, their tightly knit community had become a virtual republic in its own right. But increasing contact with – and later reliance on – the mainland in the nineteenth and twentieth centuries gradually eroded their independence until evacuation became inevitable.

What their lives had been like for century after century, why they left, and what happened to them afterwards is the subject of Tom Steel's fascinating book. It is the story of a way of life unlike any other, told here in words and pictures, and of how the impact of 'civilization' finally led to its death.

'. . . first-rate recreation of a vanished way of life'
The Scotsman

'. . . compulsive reading'
The Guardian

INTO UNKNOWN ENGLAND 1866-1913

SELECTIONS FROM THE SOCIAL EXPLORERS

Edited by Peter Keating

How did the poor live in late Victorian and Edwardian England?
In the slums of London and Birmingham? In the iron-town of
Middlesbrough? In a Devon fishing village? In rural Essex?

This is a fascinating sequence of extracts from the writings of
those individuals, journalists and wealthy businessmen, a
minister's wife, and a popular novelist, who temporarily left the
comfort of their middle-class homes to find out how the other
half lived. Peter Keating includes material from Charles Booth,
Jack London, B. S. Rowntree and C. F. G. Masterman as well as
by such lesser-known figures as George Sims, Andrew Mearns
and Stephen Reynolds.

'. . . a brilliant and compelling anthology . . . *Into Unknown
England* is not only an education in itself, throwing into three-
dimensional chiaroscuro the flat statistics of "scientific" history,
but a splendid example of prose which is always immediate and
alive.'
Alan Brien, *Spectator*

'The writers collected here used all the techniques they could to
solicit sympathy. Their descendants are a thousand television
documentaries.'
Paul Barker, *The Times*

'. . . a rich collection of passages, intelligently presented.'
The Guardian

Fontana Paperbacks: Non-fiction

Fontana is a leading paperback publisher of non-fiction, both popular and academic. Below are some recent titles.

You can buy Fontana paperbacks at your local bookshop or newsagent. Or you can order them from Fontana Paperbacks, Cash Sales Department, Box 29, Douglas, Isle of Man. Please send a cheque, postal or money order (not currency) worth the purchase price plus 10p per book (or plus 12p per book if outside the UK).

NAME (Block letters)

ADDRESS